The Almost Legendary
Morris Sisters

The

Almost
Legendary
Morris Sisters

{ A TRUE STORY
of FAMILY FICTION }

Julie Klam

RIVERHEAD BOOKS
NEW YORK
2021

RIVERHEAD BOOKS
An imprint of Penguin Random House LLC
penguinrandomhouse.com

Grateful acknowledgment is made for permission to reprint the following:

"A Needle in a Haystack"
Words by Herbert Magidson, Music by Con Conrad
© 1934 WC MUSIC CORP. (ASCAP)
All rights reserved
Used by permission of Alfred Music

Photographs of Focșani synagogue and Synagogue Râmnicu Sărat
copyright © Centropa/Daniel Gruenfeld
Photograph of Paul Koditschek courtesy of the Koditschek family
Other photos courtesy of the author

Library of Congress Cataloging-in-Publication Data

Names: Klam, Julie, author.
Title: The almost legendary Morris sisters : a true story of
family fiction / Julie Klam.
Identifiers: LCCN 2020057447 (print) | LCCN 2020057448 (ebook) |
ISBN 9780735216426 (hardcover) | ISBN 9780735216440 (ebook)
Subjects: LCSH: Morris, Selma, 1893-1991. | Morris, Malvina, 1900-1994. |
Morris, Marcella, 1901-1997. | Morris, Ruth, 1904-1978. | Morris family. |
Romanian Americans—New York (State)—New York—Biography. |
Jewish women—New York (State)—New York—Biography. |
Jews—Missouri—Saint Louis—History—20th Century—Biography.
Classification: LCC F128.9.R8 K53 2021 (print) |
LCC F128.9.R8 (ebook) | DDC 974.7/10430922 [B]—dc23
LC record available at https://lccn.loc.gov/2020057447
LC ebook record available at https://lccn.loc.gov/2020057448

Printed in the United States of America
1st Printing

Book design by Meighan Cavanaugh

For my parents

Contents

Though, it's like looking for a needle in a haystack
Still I'll follow every little clue
For I've got to find you
Although I've lost you, we'll meet again, I know

It's just like looking for a needle in a haystack
Searching for a moonbeam in the blue
Still, I've got to find you

It's just like looking for a raindrop in the ocean
Searching for a dew drop, in the dew

Still I'll follow every little clue.
For I've got to find you . . .

—*Ruth Etting, "A Needle in a Haystack"*

YSIRAEL AND RACHEL SCHNEIRER

(A partial family tree)

Rebecca Schneirer

Rachel Schneirer = Samuel Berkowitz

Martha Schneirer = Samuel Khaner

Benjamin Berkowitz = Sarah Clamer

Edward Khaner

Blanche Khaner

Nicholas Khaner

Billie Khaner = William Klam

Ruth Berkowitz

Robert Berkowitz = Eileen Novick

Claire Berkowitz

Herbert Khaner

Paul Klam = Marcia Smith

David Green

Stuart Berkowitz

Sherie Berkowitz

Carole Berkowitz

Brian Klam

Matthew Klam

Julie Klam

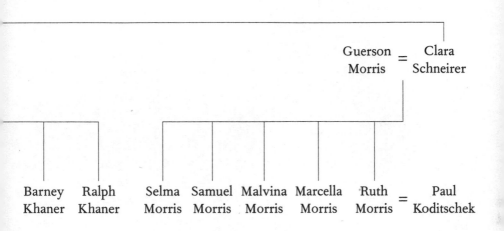

Guerson Morris = Clara Schneirer

Barney Khaner Ralph Khaner Selma Morris Samuel Morris Malvina Morris Marcella Morris Ruth Morris = Paul Koditschek

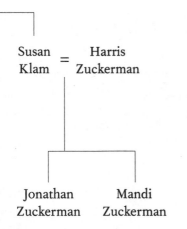

Susan Klam = Harris Zuckerman

Jonathan Zuckerman Mandi Zuckerman

A Guide to the Morris Sisters

SELMA MORRIS: The eldest. Born in November 1893 in Romania. Died in Southampton, New York, in May of 1991. Talked incessantly, was bossy, chain-smoker, very pretty with a beautiful singing voice. She spent most of her life working as a saleslady for various stores in New York City. Never married.

MALVINA MORRIS: Born March 11, 1899, in Romania. Died January 17, 1994, in Southampton. Physically disabled since childhood due to a birth defect. Was known as the kindest of the sisters, worked as a book-keeper. Chain-smoker. Never married.

MARCELLA MORRIS: Born September 30, 1901, in Romania. Died August 18, 1997, in Southampton. A financial wizard, prickly personality. Chain-smoker. Never married.

RUTH MORRIS: Born February 15, 1904, in St. Louis, Missouri. Died in January of 1978 in Southampton. The youngest and the only member of the family born in the United States. Considered bohemian, writer, was once married briefly. First of the sisters to die.

A Note on Names and Dates

A brother, Samuel Morris, born in 1897 in Romania, was the only boy and lived most of his life in Texas.

It is inevitable in genealogical research that you come across inconsistencies with names and dates. I have tried my best to keep the information in this book accurate, but there were times when someone spelled a name differently or misremembered a date. In my research, I came across the Morris sisters' father's name written as Gershon Bernhart, Gerson, Guerson, Bernhard, and George Bernard. I decided to be consistent by just using Guerson because I believe that is how it was spelled in Romania, but you'll see that in various places other people call him George or Gershon. And dates varied a great deal. This Guide to the Morris Sisters includes the dates I've determined to be correct, because they are the ones that appeared most often. (It's also where I landed on eeny, meeny, miny, moe.)

The Almost Legendary
Morris Sisters

ONE

I'd Like to Introduce My Family

When I was five years old, I noticed that my second toe was longer than my other toes. I noticed this because my grandma Billie, my father's mother, had pointed out how beautiful her own feet were because her toes were "graduated"—they were sized in ascending order. Then she looked at my feet and was silent.

Later, I mentioned to my mother what Grandma Billie had said, and she replied with extraordinary conviction, "People who have a long second toe are descended from royalty." My mother, I realized later, also has a long second toe. We were the Queen and the Princess of the Land of Goofy Feet.

At the time, I was young enough and unworldly enough that I accepted her explanation. And I knew instinctively that it wasn't something I was to talk about with other people; I didn't need to flaunt my superior lineage. I just kept the information in my back pocket, like an undercover detective with a hidden badge. If I needed to reveal it, I could, but mostly it was enough for *me* to know.

I've never taken a DNA test or any of the other tests available, mostly because I don't really care to know what someone else finds in me. I'm descended from royalty; does anything else really matter?

I'm willing to admit that I might not be Queen Elizabeth's distant cousin, but somewhere inside me that little fact—along with many, many other questionable details I was told about my family growing up—floats around in my personal identity orbit and gives me a gentle pat on the back when life gets tricky. It's okay when my credit card gets declined; I am descended from royalty.

When a friend of mine found out that her husband had been having affairs for seventeen of the eighteen years they were together—through four pregnancies and years of romantic vacations—she had the most difficult time reconciling the life she thought she'd led with the one she'd actually had. And also, reconciling herself with the fact that if she'd never found out, her life would have felt as it always had. It was the discovery that changed it. When I was younger I told my brothers that when our parents eventually died, no one should tell me for as long as possible. Let me go on and pretend that they just were too busy to pick up the phone. Maybe even record a few messages to leave for me every now and again. I clearly feel as if what I don't know can't make me sad.

It's not that I feel like I need to be protected from bad news . . . well, maybe it is that.

I think about that a lot—about how much of what defines us at various points in our lives is based on what we are told by the people we trust. Growing up, I had friends who told me they had exotic or interesting backgrounds—that they were part Sioux or Cherokee (hello, Cher? though we were just friends in my head), or that their parents once spent the evening in a New York City nightclub with Muhammad Ali and his wife, or that a friend's mother had gone trick-or-treating with Judy Garland when they were kids. And the family lore I grew up around—the strange people my relatives knew or the exciting places they'd visited, some of which turned out to be true, a lot of which turned out to be embellished, most of which was definitely curated—all goes into how we present ourselves, our lives, and our pasts to the world.

As a young kid, I was a so-so athlete (so, so terrible), and I did almost comically poorly in school ("I just don't understand how you can get a negative grade on an exam," my father once said). I wasn't conscious of the fact that other kids in sixth grade showered and washed their hair regularly until a girl in my class said for Valentine's Day she was going to give me a heart-shaped bottle of Head & Shoulders. (She did not.) So while I was often oblivious to the world around me, I knew that secretly I was very special. (Maybe it was the royal feet.)

In my defense, we were a weird family. We lived in a town where some of the people were Waspy publishers and senior vice presidents of banks, and others owned the local hardware store or drove the school bus. Their kids, my peers, were not Jewish, and their parents did not come from New York City. And the kids whose parents were bankers went to private school and I didn't, so I didn't really mix with them except during tennis and riding lessons (I know how it sounds, but trust me, I was the worst one, and remember I had the greasy hair), and the kids I went to school with were all in church together. So I sort of felt like an outsider in two places.

In college (I got into one!), I found out I had a learning disability. Maybe I hadn't been so dumb or lazy in high school, and even though I hadn't been good at sports like field hockey—or anything with a ball, really—I started running and going to the gym and found that if I worked at it consistently, I was actually pretty strong and fast. (Give me that President's Physical Fitness Test *now*!) Fortunately, this all occurred when I was young enough to incorporate these notions and changes in my behavior into my life.

After college, I came to the conclusion that I was not really good at working. I found a job working for a judgmental, hostile gentleman who criticized me constantly—so much so, in fact, that I assumed I was just terrible at my job. As I watched my friends begin to climb the ladders in their fields, earning more money and more responsibility, I was working at an insurance company and taking writing workshops on the side. I submitted one piece to a magazine, it was rejected, and I then decided that I wasn't good enough to make a career as a writer. I was always quick to allow myself to be defined by failures. Those somehow made sense to me. The women in my family succeeded in more traditional senses—cooks, homemakers, mothers. And based on what I knew about my family and history, it was what I expected for myself. That was my family narrative. But it's possible to learn something new about yourself or your family that changes the perspective and the narrative.

Every family has stories. Some people grow up hearing about their ancestors who were heroic or died violently. The accused Salem witch. The pioneer who lost a leg to frostbite but managed to walk four hundred miles to settle his family and strike gold. Families who immigrated from Ireland or India, and the people who were not brought here by choice. All of these tales go into how we define ourselves. Are we from hardworking peasant stock or from enslavers? Do we live where our ancestors did or are we scattered all over? How does knowing where we are from inform who we are now?

I heard a lot of stories growing up about my great-grandparents who came from exotic distant lands, Russia, Moldova, Bessarabia (which sounded very Aladdin-like to me), but the one story that stuck with me was an unusual one about the Morris sisters. They were, the family lore had it, four sisters who came to America sometime in the last century and were orphaned in the Midwest but somehow managed to get to New York City and become millionaires—without relying on any man—and lived in one house together. I thought of them as my great-aunts, but actually they were my paternal grandmother's first cousins, so technically they are my first cousins twice removed.

The story fascinated me; I had never heard anything like it before. It was as if the four sisters from *Little Women* had somehow been reimagined in the twentieth century and banding together had become wealthy through their own talents and ambitions. When I was a kid, I imagined they were Rich Uncle Pennybags from Monopoly, or in this case Rich Aunt Pennybags whose lives were luxurious, interesting, and sparkly. It took me forty years to realize that only one of those adjectives was true.

It turned out there was as much, if not more, misinformation about the Morris sisters as there were facts. People who grow up in the twenty-first century with so much information immediately available to them might have difficulty imagining how it was possible for everyone—in this case, everyone in an extended family—to misremember, misunderstand, or misconstrue so many details about members of their own family. How could so many intelligent people throughout a family tree have so many verifiable facts so wrong? I actually understand it pretty well. Memory is funny. What we hear, what our brain chooses to highlight, is part of it. And if you hear something you aren't familiar with, your brain might turn it into something familiar. You can get a smattering of facts and piece them together, not even realizing you're filling in blanks with your own imagination.

I would learn that finding the truth in a family can be tricky.

For example, in 1999, when my grandfather died, my father had to get his birth certificate for New York State to issue his death certificate. My father called the office of records in New York City and talked to a man who worked in the department—that's what you did at the time to get information. The man wrote down my grandfather's name and put the phone down (my dad heard shuffling and file cabinet drawers opening in the background). Five minutes later the man returned to the phone to tell my father that he had a paper copy of my grandfather's birth certificate. All of my father's life the one detail he knew for certain about his father was that his birthday was on Halloween, October 31. To my brothers and me, this was significant, because we were children and Halloween was among the most fun days of the year.

Only it wasn't true. My grandfather's real birthday was November 9, nine days after Halloween. It's not as if my grandfather had a secret wife or a hidden family, but learning this shocked my family. The truth can do that.

Several years before that I was a sophomore in college, and I remember sitting at my aunt Mattie's dining room table in Manhattan, thumbing through an ASCAP magazine (that is the American Society of Composers, Authors and Publishers). Something in the magazine must have jogged my memory, as I mentioned to her that I was related to Irving Berlin.

She came out of the kitchen and looked at me.

"Who in your father's family is related to Irving Berlin?" she asked.

(There might have been a subtext of "who in your father's loser

family was related to one of the greatest composers of all time?"
She loves my father, but she was suspicious that his tone-deaf family could be related to the man responsible for "White Christmas.")

"Not my father," I declared, *my mother!*"

She blinked at me a few times.

"If my sister is related to Irving Berlin, then I am related to Irving Berlin," Aunt Mattie said. "And I'm not related to Irving Berlin."

We immediately called my mother, and she and Mattie got into one of those conversations that sisters do, which run along the lines of "wasn't Aunt Rae's cousin's wife . . ." And lo, it turned out that my mother was wrong. I was no more related to Irving Berlin than I was to Julius Erving.

My mother wasn't embarrassed or upset when she realized she was wrong. "I guess I was thinking of someone else," she said.

Perhaps we were related to a different Irving Berlin, or the Irving who owned a discount furniture store in Berlin, Ohio.

"Well, we were related to Hartz Mountain!" Mom said proudly.

So now I'd go back to the five million people I'd told I was related to the great American songwriter and tell them that I'm not related to Irving Berlin but actually to the flea prevention people. Or maybe I wouldn't because I had always loved my quirky, cool pedigree. So what if it wasn't true? Who was going to find out?

That conversation was way back in 1985, before the World Wide Web was born, so at the time a lot of stories about family and ancestry were taken at face value. When someone told me he was related to Elizabeth Cady Stanton, I couldn't ask for proof from Ancestry.com, so I didn't ask for any documentation. I just believed him. And as a kid if my parents said we were one-eighth Inuit, I would assume that they were telling the truth, just as I assumed my relative had written "God Bless America" because my mother had once mentioned it.

I'm sure we all know people who have dazzling (or at least interesting) stories about their lineage. Your grandfather's cousin who was the captain of the *Mauretania*. Your mother's best friend who was Theda Bara's makeup artist, Persian royalty, or Irving Berlin. It was always lovely to hear these stories, and the only necessary reaction is to just say, "Wow."

Why are these stories from our families so flawed? Many reasons. Oral history is not unlike a game of telephone: Even when people are trying to get the story right, it gets twisted in unexpected ways—and not necessarily in the ways we think. One detail you hear a lot when someone is investigating their family is that their family's name was changed when they immigrated—at Ellis Island, for example—because the clerks didn't speak the language of the immigrant and wrote down whatever name they felt like. My grandfather told me his grandfather had been named Kuperschmidt, but the Ellis Island officials (he had a less polite term for them) changed it to Smith.

But this is not actually true. When people came through Ellis Island during the sixty-two years that it was open as an immigration station, the only information the immigration clerks had was the steamship's manifest with the names of the incoming immigrants. These had been filled in by the ship's officials in the originating country, who spoke the language. The Ellis Island clerks, with the aid of an interpreter, asked each entrant questions to verify they were the people on the manifest. It is true that some names were changed, but often it was done by the immigrants themselves before they left their country. Some of them may have wanted to sound more American when they got here. Or they felt a certain spelling made it easier for people. Whatever the reason, a changed name wasn't because of a lazy admission clerk at Ellis Island. Yet you hear people repeating this story all the time.

My other grandfather had been born Louis Klam and changed his name to William Klam because he had been arrested for bootlegging on the Lower East Side of Manhattan. (To be honest, there were times in my life when I might have changed Klam, but now I'm glad he didn't.) His wife, Ida, changed her name to Billie because she thought it sounded more glamorous. Ida/Billie's sister Rebecca became Blanche because it was modern; her brother Israel became Stanley, and then finally settled on Edward. People often reinvented themselves with names the same way they'd change their hairstyle or wear a new hat. I think of it as the old-fashioned version of changing your avatar.

But the Morris sisters, my father's mother's cousins, were real people. Ever since I was young, they were legendary members of my family. I was told they were completely crazy, obscenely wealthy, never married, had no children, and all lived together in a house in New York City. Selma, Malvina, Marcella, and Ruth Morris. I grew up listening to my grandmother's fascinating, somewhat questionable, and often inconsistent stories of these women, who were her first cousins. The common thread in the stories was that every one of my father's family had a story to tell about them, most involving how much money they gave to Brandeis University and how little they gave to [fill in relative's name who is telling the story].

I actually met Malvina and Marcella Morris in the summer of 1980 when I was thirteen, at my grandparents' fiftieth anniversary party. My grandma Billie, who was a little on the vain side, told Marcella and me how she modeled for her father, a dress designer in the 1920s, because she was a perfect size 5 and remained a size 5 all of her life.

Marcella, taller than my four-foot-eleven-inch grandmother, but not by much, with short gray hair and no makeup, and stinking of cigarette smoke, dressed in polyester pants with a matching vest and long-sleeve shirt, said, "That's 'cause they make that stretchy fabric now!" And then she took a long drag on her Pall Mall.

My family did just fine. We had everything we wanted, but I never thought of us as rich. We didn't have servants and our dinner didn't come on silver platters with lids that were lifted by a butler. The Morris sisters were that kind of rich, or so I was led to believe. I imagined that if I'd had a chance to meet all of them they'd be charmed by my brilliance and my sense of humor, and one of them would pull out a ribbon-tied scroll of parchment and unroll it to reveal the word "WILL" at the top of the page, and with a feather quill she would scratch out whoever's name was written on it and put in "our dear cousin Julie Klam," leaving everything the sisters had to me.

I had wanted to meet Marcella even before the party. She was, the story went, the sister who had made all the money. I had heard the Morris sisters only liked girls. (I didn't know at the time what a lesbian was, so I assumed it was more misandry.) When I finally did meet her, I attempted to dazzle her with my intellect and wit. But apparently she wasn't impressed, because she walked away without saying a word to me or giving me a dime. And her purse wasn't big enough for a scroll.

I didn't think much about the Morris sisters until a couple of years later when I visited my father's cousin Claire in the Florida Keys.

My dad's family had a cousins' club: Almost every year most of his first cousins and their families would congregate at someone's house for a visit. It was a way for us all to stay in contact. We had many of them at our house in Westchester County, New York, north of New York City, and at these get-togethers Claire always sought me out. I was the youngest child in my family, and at the time my brothers didn't have a lot of use for me except if I wanted to be the backboard and hoop of their basketball game. (They were pretty horrible, but the good news is I've spent most of my adult life making them pay.) Claire related to this and she was always on my side for the time we were together. She didn't ask me the typical questions that adults do about how old I was or what was my favorite subject in school. Instead she'd tell me stories about how she'd had an annoying cousin when she was younger, and spent a lot of time plotting her death. She was my kind of relative.

When Claire invited me to the Keys, I jumped at it. She was maybe fifty, a little older than my parents, but she was fun with a capital *F*. She took me deep-sea fishing and then, with a guide, into the backcountry of the Everglades, where we fed marshmallows to a one-eyed alligator named Andy.

Claire was married to Jerry, but he was often in New Jersey working, and her two daughters were adults with children of their own. She had lived a pretty traditional life, getting married and staying at home with her children. When I knew her, she was at a point in her life where she was figuring out what she wanted to do next.

During my visit, Claire also invited her adult friends to the Keys. One was a single man with two sons. At every chance she got, Claire would challenge them to contests against us—boys against girls. Fishing (the biggest fish, the most fish caught, the first catch), tennis, swimming. Whatever the challenge was, somehow, Claire and I always won. And Claire rubbed it in with a delicious vigor.

In the evenings at sunset she and I would sit on the docks and watch the seabirds dovening, she with a glass of wine and I with a Tab, and she'd tell me about the Morrises. Selma was the oldest. When she was young, she was very beautiful and had a

Selma Morris

glorious singing voice, but when she was older, when Claire knew her, she just drove everyone crazy. She never stopped talking. "I remember very clearly when my father and his brother took Selma to Montreal to visit the family," Claire said. (The third sister of my great-grandmother Martha and the Morris sisters' mother, Clara, was Rebecca, who had settled in Montreal.) "I remember my mother was with us. The only reason they took Selma was to pay for the gas. Halfway there they could not stand her talking and complaining, so they threw her out of the car!" She laughed. "It was in Watertown, New York. She really was impossible to be with for any length of time. She only wanted to stop at a restaurant for a nice barbecued hamburger with lettuce and tomatoes, and don't forget the onions! And the french fries—very well done!"

Malvina was the second sister; she had a childhood illness that left her with one leg shorter than the other and a pretty significant limp. She was known to be the sweetest and kindest, and was adored by everyone. She worked in administrative jobs and stuck closely to her sisters. She was also a very gifted painter.

Marcella, the third, was the financier. She was fiercely independent and a genius with numbers. It was her intense determination that got the girls to New York, where she then had an incredibly successful financial career. She had short hair and wore pants the minute it became acceptable. She had a deep dislike of men.

Ruth was the baby. Claire said, "Ruth was really very pretty and totally bohemian. She wrote beautiful stories and was a painter. She was the only person I know who wore high button shoes, bloomers, and very flared skirts with a stiff crinoline to hold the skirt—and this was in the 1950s and '60s! All the sisters swore that Ruth wrote the musical *High Button Shoes*, but she told me that a Broadway producer who came on to her stole the script. Julie, I believe it. She showed me the script she wrote. She certainly dressed the part. I wish I had saved some of Ruth's stories. You would have loved them. I remember when she came to my house for Thanksgiving one year, with her high button shoes and her crazy outfit. She asked my kids if they could stand on their heads, and with that she stood on her head, and that's how we knew she wore bloomers. She was in her sixties then!"

I'd heard from my father that Ruth wore a lot of brightly colored silk scarves and noisy jewelry and that she had painted her fingernails a dark purple and that in her bag she carried a perfume atomizer with a bulb sprayer and that the scent was called something exotic like 1001 Arabian Nights. "Oh," Claire said, "they all smoked like chimneys! I mean a lot of people smoked then, but they *smoked*."

Claire spoke of them as funny and unusual and brave. She

envied their independence from men. We sat quietly for a time, both reflecting on these amazing women as the sun dipped into the Gulf of Mexico.

In 1993, my brother Matthew had his first short story published in *The New Yorker,* followed by several others. With his tremendous acclaim, he officially became the writer in the family. One day, Matt received a cassette tape in the mail. It was from Claire.

He put it in his tape deck and we heard her voice with its inimitable New Jersey accent declare: "The Morris Sisters: An Impossible Dream."

There was Claire, on Memorex, telling the whole story of the Morris sisters as she knew it, and more important, her own stories of her experiences with the Morrises. Claire may not have been a writer, but she was one of the best storytellers I ever knew. She would sit at a table and every head would be facing her, mouth open, ready to gasp or laugh.

With each story the sisters became clearer in our minds—more vivid, more three-dimensional. The stories Claire told about them made them into real people. When people find out you're a writer, they tell you what they think is a great idea for a book, a magazine article, a TV show, a movie, or a miniseries. It doesn't matter what you write or where your interest lies, it's not about you: It's their great idea, and they are giving it to you. Every time my grandpa Willie saw Matt, he would tell him he should write a book about how his son (our father) retired at age fifty-five. (Matt's stories are about sexuality and infidelity, and they use a lot of *F* words. They don't tend to be about retirement.) I was writing then, too, but short reported pieces for *Rolling Stone* and *Us* magazines. (I was also writing screenplays for no one.) While I was still employed at the insurance company, I had no idea what I was going to do professionally. My ambition was to be not working at the insurance company forever, but at that point that was the extent of my career planning. I thought I was a writer, but I never imagined I would be able to make a living as a writer (which was actually pretty prescient of me). Still, I loved Claire so much that when I heard her stories about the Morris sisters, I wanted that tape for myself. Not to do anything with it, just to have it.

My brother, being a generous sort, gave it to me. I listened to it a few times, absorbing Claire's stories. I kept the tape with my other cassettes until tapes were no more, and then I threw all of them away, and now they're gone forever.

In 2008, I published my first book, *Please Excuse My Daughter,* a memoir about my mother and me and how I grew up, and it dipped a little into my mother's family's history, which was rich and interesting. Her mother's uncle, Sam Golding, developed the neighborhood of Rego Park in Queens during the 1920s. In fact, I had always been told that the name Rego Park was for my mother's grandmother RosE GOlding, but in every documented story about the history of the name, it's said to come from Real Good Construction Company. When I told that to my mom and Aunt Mattie, they said everyone was wrong, they were certain the family story is true. End of story.

There are buildings and hospitals around New York City that still bear his name. Once at my parents' house, I found a bag of yarmulkes from various weddings and bar mitzvahs. One was from Sam's daughter Faith's wedding to Ronald O. Perelman, the Revlon tycoon who went on to marry Claudia Cohen, Patricia Duff, Ellen Barkin, and Anna Chapman. But his first wedding in 1965 was to *my* relative. (All of this information was in my book. While I used the internet to research it, it was different then: Google wasn't a verb yet, and a lot fewer documents were available online.) I looked through old New York City phone books—actual physical phone books—found people's addresses, and interviewed the people who were still alive at that time, and though I couldn't always verify their stories, it was fine. It was a memoir, not a history book, after all. I loved the quest for information about my family, though: It was like searching for buried treasure and actually thinking there was a decent chance I would find it. The feeling I had poring over the names of the 1943 Manhattan phone book and finding my grandfather's office address and telephone number was like I had time traveled. In 1943, he was alive, and people who wanted to talk to him looked up his telephone number in that phone book and called him at his office. A secretary answered, and eventually they got to my grandpa.

When I finished my memoir, I thought the next logical project would be a book about the Morris sisters. I had written about my mother and her family, and now I had this fascinating piece of my father's family to investigate. I'd heard about these "manless," independent, rich sisters who existed in a time when the world did not support any of that. Who were they? How did they do what they did? They were kind of radicals. Did any of what made them tick exist in me? I was trying to be more independent in my marriage, and maybe knowing how they did it would help me. They were celebrities in our family instead of being "famous" in the world like Irving Berlin. I needed to know who these women in my family *were*.

I started researching them, but it didn't take me long to realize that for women who were so famous within my family, there didn't seem to be much written about them in the world. Not to mention the fact that their last name, Morris, was extremely common, and they had lived in New York City, which isn't exactly Bedford Falls. (This was around the time Ruth Etting's "A Needle in a Haystack" became my theme song. It stayed in my head for three years.)

I started my research by interviewing first Claire and then her older brother, Bobby. While their stories were helpful, they were only a start. I needed more. To really find, understand, and tell the story of the Morris sisters, I would need to dig deeper than anecdotes, to go beyond the family lore to the places where they had lived and where their family had come from and generally *look for things* (to use a technical genealogy term). My agent, publisher, and editor were all on board.

There were problems, though. My then husband and I didn't have much money, and we had a child in kindergarten who needed a lot of attention (as opposed to the self-cleaning, autonomous models). My husband was freelancing, and his jobs required very long days and frequent travel. We couldn't both be working full days and traveling a lot, so I put aside the idea for a book about the Morris sisters and wrote a book about dog rescue instead, an activity I was doing anyway. (The dogs were on a different side of my family.) As I began to write my second book about dogs, it was evident that my marriage was not going to make it. I went on to write a book about friendship, and while I was writing that book, my husband and I began the lengthy, exhausting process of getting divorced. So it was one step forward (the child got older) and two steps back (I was now a single parent with even less money than before).

During these years, I had been writing a book a year as well as other pieces for magazines. With all that was happening in my life, it was now taking almost three years to write what became my fifth book. It was about the nature of celebrity, which sounded like a good idea because it wasn't about me: I was at a point in my life where the last subject I wanted to write about was myself. Except I had a really hard time doing it: I became a kind of champion at not writing my book. I would fantasize about having the kind of job you left the house for and sat at a desk and people gave you tasks to complete—much as I did when I worked at the life insurance company. I envied anyone who knew what they were supposed to be doing, and I would grill people about the stresses of their jobs. (It turns out the only jobs with no stress are the ones *you* aren't doing.)

Somehow the book got written and published, my divorce was finalized, and I found myself in the magical place of deciding what to write next. It's such an amazing place to be because you can choose where you want to go for the next two or three years. It's all possible and every idea in your mind is an instant classic/billion seller. Do I want to write about real-life wizards or haunted houses or spelunking? Well, no. I had several conversations with friends and one with my good friend Ann Leary, who told me about the research she'd been doing on Ancestry and the amazing information she'd learned about her family. Ann is someone who doesn't do anything halfway, so by the time we talked, she was already an expert in family searches. I told her about my long-abandoned task to write about the Morris sisters. She pointed out that the internet had changed since I first thought about this book and that more and more information was becoming public and available. So she said, "Do it!"

"Maybe," I said. And then I went to the gym.

While I was there, Ann started texting me all of the details she was discovering about the Morrises on Ancestry.com. She was right: The details were intriguing, and there was much more information about them than Claire and Bobby had told me several years ago.

Sometime on the StairMaster while I was trying to ignore *The Price Is Right*, a book about the Morris sisters seemed possible, and something that I could get really excited about.

I went home and pulled out the old proposal and found that I had taken a lot of notes and had a small folder of research. It had been ten years—ten really difficult years. Divorce, anxiety, and insomnia, too many glasses of sauvignon blanc. All of this left my brain a little worse for wear, but the good news was that the story of the Morris sisters still felt new to me. I was still fascinated by what I had found and intrigued by the possibilities of what I could find that lay in front of me. It began to feel that I couldn't not write this book.

When you start researching family, well-meaning people direct you to genealogists. As with most vocations, there are amateurs and professionals, and they are all similarly driven: They are the experts at digging for information about your ancestors and family. This, I have learned, is a double-edged sword.

I have always felt that the copy editors who have worked on my books and magazine pieces have a genetic makeup fundamentally different than mine: Their brains operate on a different wavelength. They notice mistakes and inconsistencies that in a thousand years I never would have found. I have the same feeling about genealogists. They think differently than I do. They keep looking even when they're not finding anything and it seems that they won't learn anything new about the people you want information about.

Someone I talked to early on in the research for this book told me that genealogy is just a series of paths that lead to brick walls. "Brick wall," I learned, is actually a very common term you hear in genealogy. I am not a genealogist. (It's taken me three years to spell it without looking it up.) I am not a researcher. (I research people and topics the same way my child looks for something he can't find in his room, sort of a fast scan of a large space and then falling to the floor in defeat.) I came to this conclusion about myself when I spent several hours at the New York Public Library trying to track down information about the Morris sisters and the only useful detail I was able to find that day was the location of the bathroom. And I was so psyched about it.

And although I've written for newspapers and magazines, I'm not really a journalist. I don't like bothering people. If I call a source and the person doesn't respond right away, I quietly assume the information can't be found.

I straddle two mindsets. I grew up without the internet, so when I was young if I wanted to find something, I went to the library. If I wanted to find a word within a document, I read the whole document as carefully as I could looking for the word. It was a slow, step-by-step process.

But now I—and everyone else—live in the world where it's possible to locate just about any piece of information immediately in the palm of my hand, which suits my short attention span well. As soon as you start even a cursory exploration into your family's past, you see inconsistencies. Names and dates and places change throughout the records. In one place it might say a person was born in London, and in another it says Liverpool. My point is that genealogical records are neither a straight line nor consistent. Like a lot of life, it's open to interpretation.

For example, not a single one of the US Census records I found in my investigation of the Morris sisters spelled their names correctly. Some of the records didn't even list them at all. Each sister had about five different dates of birth. People of their time may have taken down the information correctly, but I couldn't be certain that the Mormon librarian who read the information from these handwritten documents typed them correctly into genealogical databases.

From the very beginning I understood the difficulties I faced. As a writer and essayist, I'm resourceful at finding information when I know it's out there, but when I wanted to get to know the Morris sisters by researching their lives, I was aware that I was not going to be able to find everything I needed or wanted to know. It's literally impossible. A lot of genealogical information comes from census reports, and they aren't available to the public until seventy-two years after they are taken. The law governing this, passed in 1978, was an outgrowth of an agreement between the Census Bureau and the National Archives. For privacy reasons, access to personally identifiable information in US Census records is restricted unless you're the one in the record or their legal heir. So, at the time of this writing (2020), the census data available took me up to only the 1940s. The last Morris sister, Marcella, died in 1997.

So it's a shame not to know more because census information can neatly define someone's life. But unless I want to wait another ten or twenty years, I have to contend with what's available. And I know that there are always going to be limitations to what we can know about the past and our ancestors, and in the future I know I will have more information—census reports and beyond—but at the same time then there will be fewer people around who will remember the sisters. Trying to find the truth in your family is a balancing act between learning facts and learning what people thought.

As I read over what I've written here so far, I realize that it meanders and hits several "brick walls" that genealogists talk about. Those experiences turn out to be pretty accurate metaphors for the journey I went on to learn and write about the Morris sisters. Their stories didn't turn out the way I expected: What happened to them and what happened to me as I learned about them startled and unsettled me, and it took me to places and introduced me to people I never expected to meet. In the end the search made me reconsider how families tell the stories of the people they're related to in order to make sense of the world and the legacy they left. And the Morris sisters were about to add a very different chapter to my own story.

TWO

What I Don't Know Could
Fill a Book

As far as I knew it from my family, the story of the Morris sisters was this:

In 1900, George and Clara Morris and their four children, Samuel, Selma, Marcella, and Malvina, left Bucharest, Romania, and boarded a ship for New York City. When they arrived in the United States, they stayed in New York City for a few weeks and then decided to move to Los Angeles, where George wanted to become a director in the movie business. Along the way, in St. Louis, Clara had another baby and died in childbirth. George put the children in an orphanage there before heading on to Los Angeles, where he promised to send for them. The children stayed in the orphanage until the oldest child, Marcella, was able to make enough money to get them all out. She moved them back to New

York City, where she became the first Jewish female to hold a seat on the Wall Street stock exchange, where she made millions of dollars that she later gave to Brandeis University. She lived with her sisters in an apartment on Charles Street in Greenwich Village and had a house in Southampton, New York, and somewhere along the way had an affair with J. P. Morgan.

Interesting? You bet. But don't worry about remembering any of this, because it's 90 percent wrong, which I didn't find out until years later.

I DECIDED THAT my first plan of attack would be to uncover information about Marcella Morris and J. P. Morgan. I figured that, being the richest man in the world at the time, Morgan had plenty written about him over the years and that tracking down his connection to Marcella and the Morris sisters would be possible, maybe even fairly simple.

In the early 1990s, my friend Jancee and I would often meet at the Morgan Library on Madison Avenue, where we'd have a proper English tea with sandwiches and scones and lemon cookies. The Morgan Library is an astonishingly beautiful building inside and out, and its permanent collection includes a Gutenberg Bible, some of Mozart's original compositions, a Rubens, a collection of Henry David Thoreau's notes, and other priceless treasures that Morgan had collected over the years. It also has a lot of information about J. P. Morgan himself that is available to the public.

I was sure that the Morgan Library archive would have information on Marcella and her career and possibly her affair with Morgan himself. Once I had Marcella's background clear, I could fill in the rest of the sisters' stories around that.

One day in early spring, I headed to the Morgan, where I spent several hours walking through the place looking at paintings of J. P. Morgan and searching for clues about Marcella in the public archive. I remembered that Claire had mentioned on her cassette that Marcella had decorated one of Morgan's New York City homes. Had she bought the chair that Morgan was seated in in one of the oil paintings that hung on the walls of the Morgan? It was exciting to imagine.

I read the descriptions beside each of the paintings, and I began to get a vague sense that something wasn't right with the story of Marcella and Morgan. But I brushed aside such thoughts and bought a fat biography of J. P. Morgan in the gift shop. Surely, I figured, I could get the nuts and bolts about Marcella from it, and then I'd come back to the library and talk to a research librarian.

IT PROBABLY COMES as no surprise to you that there was no mention of Marcella anywhere in the book. It was long—more than eight hundred pages—and it was full of details about Morgan's professional and personal lives. But the more of the book I read, the more I realized that it was nearly impossible that Marcella and Morgan had ever known each other—that it was more than probable that she never even met him. Even at this early point in my research, when I didn't know much about Marcella's life, I did know that she had died in her late nineties at the end of the 1990s, which meant that when J. P. Morgan died in Italy in 1913, Marcella would have been about twelve years old and living in an orphanage in St. Louis.

I spent the next few days trying hard—really hard—to fit that square peg of information into the round hole of my family's stories about Marcella. Then I had a great epiphany: They must have been talking about J. P. Morgan's son, J. P. "Jack" Morgan Jr. I stayed up all night reading so much about him that I could have written his biography, and to my crushing disappointment, nothing remotely connected him to Marcella—and believe me, I tried to make it possible. It just didn't work.

So this foundational piece of the Morris sisters story was blasted to smithereens by a giant wrecking ball of reality. I was surprised at how devastated I felt. The very first detail I looked to corroborate turned out to be absurdly off base, which made me wonder: What if none of the stories I heard about the Morris sisters were true? What was I writing? Who were these women? Was this going to be another Irving Berlin? Who was I?

THREE

The Morris Family Foundation, Inc.

I was disappointed but not discouraged. In fact, I redoubled my efforts and started emailing libraries, historical societies, and financial museums in all of the places where I knew the Morris sisters and their family had lived. I was searching for confirmation—any confirmation—about what I had been told about them.

My first response came from the Rogers Memorial Library in Southampton, New York. The head librarian there told me not only that she knew who the Morris sisters were, but also that the most popular conference room at the library was called the Morris Meeting Room after them.

When I learned that, I may have exhaled for the first time in days.

The librarian also told me there is a plaque on the wall that

commemorated their contribution to the library, and emailed me
the text:

A gift from the Morris Family Foundation, Inc., has enabled the
library to enhance this important part of the Library's services.
The gift honors the Morris sisters, Marcella, Selma, Malvina
and Ruth, who were long time residents of Southampton. As
youngsters, they were traveling across the country with their
parents who were headed toward a better life with hopes
of working in the motion picture industry in California.
Unfortunately, they were abandoned along with their brother,
Samuel, by their destitute father when their mother died in St.
Louis in the early 1920's. Raised in the Jewish Orphanage until
their early teens, the Morris children not only survived their
hardships but eventually distinguished themselves in their
careers and financial accomplishments. At age sixteen, Samuel
left the orphanage and headed for Texas where he worked to
buy his own business and live out his life in San Antonio.

Marcella, at age thirteen, convinced the orphanage to
release her so that she could earn enough money to pay the
orphanage back the $250 for each of the sisters and take care
of them herself. She went to Cleveland and became a filing
clerk in the J.P. Morgan and Company office. Her extraordinary
intelligence and memory skills earned her many promotions and
a transfer to New York. Marcella became the first woman
commodity trader in the financial world dominated by men. Her
specialties were pork bellies and winter corn and her fame was
such that during World War II she was invited to the White
House to enlighten the President and his cabinet about
worldwide supplies.

The sisters, Malvina (who suffered from polio), Selma and
Ruth were reunited through Marcella's efforts and they lived
together for the rest of their lives, working and amassing a
fortune.

The Morris sisters lived moderately and gave generously.
They were self-educated once they left the orphanage. They

read and studied widely and relied on public libraries more than on building their own collections. Each of them succeeded in their chosen fields, but it was Marcella's wealth that insured their fortune. It was her plan to take care of her sisters and try to time it so that when the last one died all the wealth had been given away to the causes they believed in. All the sisters lived together for their entire lives, and helped many people who never knew the Morris sisters or their history. The Morris Family Foundation, Inc., continues to fulfill their wishes.

We dedicate this center to them in grateful memory
Marcella Malvina Selma Ruth
1902–1995* 1899–1994 1903–1991 1904–1978

Well! This was a lot! A pretty clear biography. And also, the White House? I was breathing quite evenly now.

I asked the librarian who had written the inscription, and she sent me a longer version of the biography, which she indicated had come from "the Morris Foundation," an organization I had never heard of and I knew had never been mentioned in any of the lore about the Morris sisters that I had heard.

With so much detail, I thought this book might be *too* easy to write. (Feel free to chuckle.) If there is a foundation that had been established by the sisters and a biography about them already available, then all I would really need to do was flesh out their individual stories, add some interesting details and colorful asides, and I'd be done.

---

*Marcella's dates were actually 1901–1997 and Selma was actually born in 1893, but I didn't know that yet.

I downloaded the biography from the librarian and printed it out—two pages, single spaced. And it was a surprise from the very beginning.

Around the turn of the century, the Morris family started out on a journey from their home in Montreal, Canada, to somewhere in California. It was winter in Montreal and winters in that part of the world were cold, very cold. The mother had been treated for a well-known and much feared disease called "consumption" and many people of that period who were so afflicted did not survive the winter. Her husband was an unemployed photographer who got the idea that he should take his wife to a better climate and with the motion picture industry just getting started, it might provide opportunity for an available photographer. He just had to get an automobile big enough to fit his wife and five children ages 2 to 11; Selma, Samuel, Malvina, who was lame, Marcella and Ruth. He was in luck when he learned that his brother would lend him an old seven passenger "Pierce Arrow" automobile. So off they went on their adventure, using mostly roads and pathways that for the most part were used for horse drawn vehicles.

The journey was a lot harder than he anticipated and his wife was getting a lot worse. She had a constant cough, coughing so bad that it seemed she would explode. As the family reached St. Louis, she was put in a hospital and soon died. The father was out of money and with five very young children on his hands, thought it best to leave his children at the Jewish Orphanage on a temporary basis or until he could find a job and accumulate enough money to continue their journey. He stated to his children, "Mother would certainly want him to do this" and he promised to be back no later than the end of the month to reclaim his family.

He was not there at the end of the month, nor at the end of a hundred ensuing months; at the early months there was disappointment but the older children felt he would definitely return someday, but he never did. Soon the children got into life at the orphanage; it was clear now they had to stick together to survive this uncertainty they knew nothing about. A short time ago they had a loving mother and father and now they only had each other.

As the days went by there were new routines to learn, still at the end of each month they felt their father might be there, they would never give up, always wondering whether their father took a wrong turn, whether he was in some institution, terminally ill from some misfortunate accident, maybe he was just detained by someone or something. This became an obsession with them, years later they employed enormous resources of time and money to try and find him, but of no avail.

Sam, the oldest and only male child in their family, left the orphanage first. He was sixteen and because of hard times the Orphanage expected residents to leave at that age, get an appropriate job and pay them back the sum of $250. That was what they figured was fair for past services rendered. He headed for Texas and got a job in an Army surplus store in San Antonio. Eventually, he bought the store and spent his life living in the back room, single, keeping to himself, but always inquiring by way of a letter to his sisters asking, "What did you find out about our Papa?"

The orphanage placed Malvina with a local family in St. Louis because they claimed they could not provide care for a lame child. This stressed her sisters more than they could cope with.

Marcella had gotten a reputation of being very smart, she was barely thirteen years old, but she convinced the authorities at the orphanage to release her to go find a job, one that would pay enough money so she could pay the $250 due for each child. They expected to be paid, but as it turned out, payment was rarely forthcoming. The orphanage said, strangely, they believed her and agreed to let her go.

Marcella went to Cleveland where she got a filing job with J.P. Morgan and Company. The manager of that office soon learned he had a file clerk who read everything she filed and remembered every important fact on the filed sheets. She was remembered as the resource with a wealth of information no one else had. She was eventually transferred to their New York office where she became one of the most successful traders they ever had. Her specialty was pork bellies and winter corn. She was the only female trader then and for thirty years later. Her knowledge of pork bellies was world famous; in fact during World War II she was summoned to the White House, pork was then a diet staple for the armed forces and the then President Roosevelt wanted to be sure he knew where the world's supply was accounted for.

Marcella earned a fortune of money, lived together with her three sisters, first in an apartment on Charles Street, Manhattan, then for thirty or so years in Southampton. They lived modestly; their dealings were mostly with women, gave away huge amounts of money mostly to charities dealing with women. There is the theory of male betrayal that was suspected to have a role in all of their decision making, even though it was never proved. Many times when they were asked why they never married, they made it clear they would never trust another man. Marcella earned all the family wealth; her plan was to take care of her sisters and time it so that when the last one died, all the wealth would be given away. She almost made it.

They are all deceased now. Ruth was 86, Selma was 102, Malvina with the lame leg hopped around for 96 years, and Marcella, the last one to die just short of 97, stayed around just long enough to survive her sisters and finalize her affairs.

They had a long life, not always happy, but always their way. They were big time cigarette smokers, maybe three packs every day of their lives; ate all the wrong foods, only foods that were tasty to them: good health was never a consideration. They were well enough in mind and body so that until their last days on earth they could carry out their daily activities. They were survivors, they had a lot of hurt, but they carried on and gave a lot back to help others who never knew who the Morrises were, but it didn't matter to them because that was their way.

Though it wasn't the smoothest biography I ever read, there was a lot of information.

I called Claire and read it to her.

"Well, that's very nice," she said, "but it's fiction."

"Which part?" I asked. I was not ready to give up on this.

"Well, some of it is right. But what I know was that the

Morrises landed on Ellis Island with the plan to go to St. Louis, because their father was a concert violinist and he was going to play with the symphony there."

This was news—new news, in fact. Had the Morris sisters' father been a violinist or a photographer? How could I find out?

It was clear that I needed to divide the verifiable truth from the family fiction. It was also clear that I needed to approach this question more methodically than I had to this point.

FOUR

Step One: Index Cards

To start my journey toward greater clarity, I bought two different multicolored packs of index cards, and on the coffee table in the living room, I separated them into colors. Each color, I decided, would be assigned to a family member, and the leftover colors would be for the places they lived.

After making this determination, which felt like a significant accomplishment, I stared at the index cards for a couple of weeks without writing anything on them. Everyone in my family kept knocking them off the table, so I frequently had to re-collate.

I am telling you this because I really had no idea where to begin.

I am a great researcher of one question at a time. If you want me to find out which window air conditioner is the best one for you to buy or what mallard ducks eat in the wild, I am on it—and

I always come up with the answer. But the journey to understanding the Morris sisters and their lives traveled over a vast sea of questions, and I knew I couldn't cross it without help. I knew I needed assistance.

Putting someone's, let alone four someones', life story together is daunting. And I was fairly sure that there were tricks and tips and methods that I was not at all familiar with. When my child had to research our family for a school project, I subscribed to Ancestry .com, and we were able to find little bits of information about my and my ex-husband's grandparents, but as we only signed up for the free trial, we didn't go very far with it. When I got interested in the Morris sisters, I remembered that poking around on the site was kind of revelatory, so I paid for a new Ancestry.com membership and began to look around. There were specific tips about widening your search parameters to include more years than you might think to look at and more interpretations of how to spell the names you were trying to track down. One of Ancestry's services in particular caught my eye: Hire an Expert. It seemed like a good idea to hire someone who could find all of the elements faster and more completely than you ever could. But I wasn't ready for that yet, partly because I wasn't exactly sure what I was looking for and partly because I knew that sometimes you found information you didn't expect to discover when you looked yourself. There were times when I was looking for a needle in a haystack and instead found a key.

I started at the beginning and entered each sister's name and approximate date of birth and various spellings. I got a lot of hits, but nothing that seemed associated with them. I kept thinking that if I were a character in a movie and I'd put in the search terms, a newspaper from 1905 would spin into focus with the headline "Mother Dies in Childbirth, Father Forced to Place Children in Orphanage," and then a big story would appear, filling in all of the details—accurately this time—and I'd know everything, maybe with a nice Movietone News narration. But life is not a movie—at least mine isn't—which is why no one pays to watch me.

It was at this point that I remembered I'd once printed out some papers about the Morrises when I was on a field trip to the Ellis Island National Museum of Immigration with my child's third-grade class. I love it there. I am not a museum person. If you ever want to go to a museum, you don't want to go with me. I zoom through, because the air in there makes me feel like I'm going to pass out, and my feet get very heavy, and if I'm carrying my coat, don't ask me anything. *Anything.* But the Ellis Island National Museum of Immigration is more of an experience. We went through the doors as if we were immigrants getting off a ship, and we visited the stations they went through (all in a fraction of the time it took actual immigrants and without the confusion and overwhelming fear of being sent back to our home country, but otherwise just like them). I have been there several times since and I have never failed to be moved by the immigrants' stories. These people left what they knew—life in a big city or a tiny village, having saved for months or even years—got on a train (or sometimes walked) to a ship that would bring them across an ocean to a place they had only heard about, having no idea what lay ahead. All they had was hope. I needed months of extra therapy to get me through my move from 100th to 106th Street.

While on the field trip as a chaperone, I had searched the Ellis Island database for the Morrises. After looking through various files, I finally found the manifest of the ship they had traveled on, but only three of the children were listed. It stated that on September 12, 1902, Israel, Malvina, and Marcel (this would have been written incorrectly by someone from the shipping company before the Morrises boarded the SS *Kensington*) traveled from Southampton, England, to Ellis Island, New York City, and that they had originally come from Romania. They traveled third class (steerage).

But where were the parents and Selma? This was a question I couldn't answer then, as at that moment it was my job to make sure twenty-seven third graders weren't leaping into New York Harbor. So I printed the page of information about the Morris family (Ellis Island allows you to do that) and tucked it away. It was clear that the Morrises didn't land in Canada as the family story went. Maybe they went to Montreal after, but they had arrived through Ellis Island in New York City from England and before that, apparently, Romania.

When you are at Ellis Island now, you hear story after story about conditions aboard ships: They were often filthy, cold, damp, and dark. People were sick and half-starved and jammed together like animals. It made perfect sense to me that under these conditions, Clara would have contracted tuberculosis.

I decided that I needed to track down Clara's death certificate and see what I could learn from it. As I began my search, I ran into the problem I had frequently had with researching this book: determining what was true and who was who. Clara Morris is not exactly an exotic name. In my searches I came across a great many Clara Morrises, including a beautiful actress born in 1849 in Canada (of all places). But the one Clara Morris I was looking for would have died around the time Ruth was born, which was 1904. (In the family biography Ruth was listed as being born in 1905, but since she was born in the United States, I was able to find a copy of her birth certificate, which was actually one line of a full registry. Her name was printed in a ledger of babies who were born in February 1904 in St. Louis.) There definitely were no Clara Morrises that fit her description who died in St. Louis in 1904 or 1905. In fact, the only Clara Morris I found who seemed as if it could be her died in St. Louis in 1953. (I had a long labor, but forty-nine years?) Something wasn't adding up.

After I found Ruth's birth certificate, I started studying census records to see whom she might have lived with. Every ten years, the federal government conducts a national census of all US citizens. And seventy-two years later the government releases detailed information about what it learned. In the 1910 and 1920 censuses, the Morrises were listed, while Clara was listed with them in 1910 but not 1920, so it seemed logical that she had died somewhere

CAROLYN LEAVITT
Leave it to Carolyn.
G. A. A., 20
Round Table, '19, '20, '21
Vice-President, '21
Lunchroom Committee

MARY REICHMAN
Silence at the proper season is wisdom, and better than any speech.
Orchestra, '18, '19, '20, 21
S. B. S., '21

IRENE LA BERGE
Perseverance conquers fate.
G. A. A., '20
S. B. S., '21
Chemistry Club, '21
Ring Committee

NORMAN EVANS
Those gentle eyes!
That marcel wave!
Edison Club, '20, '21

MARCELLA MORRIS
Thoughts of great deeds are mine.
S. B. S., '20, '21

WILLIAM BIERMAN
His hair is of a good color,
An excellent color.
Tennis, '20

Marcella Morris's yearbook, 1921

between those ten years. In other words, not in childbirth with Ruth and not from tuberculosis on the SS *Kensington*.

Armed with this information, I went back to Ancestry and started to dig.

The first unquestionably accurate details I came across were Marcella's and Ruth's yearbook pages, both from 1921. I put on a Ruth Etting album and started reading.

Marcella Morris went to Soldan High School in St. Louis, a public school that at the time was known for having wealthy and predominantly Jewish students. Her senior photo is on the bottom middle of a page among six other students who look like flappers, very chic and put together with lipstick and pearls. In contrast, Marcella had natural, frizzy hair and wore round metal eyeglasses. In the photo her lips are pressed together, and she looks as if the photographer was trying to get her to smile, but she was having none of it.

I remembered that my grandmother once said that girls growing up in the early twentieth century used curling irons that were heated with coals (and could either straighten your hair or singe it right off depending on how much attention was paid). Maybe Marcella chose to have her natural curly hair, but I couldn't help feeling that the picture showed there wasn't a mother in her life to help get her ready for her school picture.

The captions under the photos were also revealing. Marcella Morris is between Norman Evans, whose quote is "Those gentle eyes! That Marcel Wave!" (even *he* used a curling iron), and

William Bierman, who went with "His hair is of a good color, An excellent color." Marcella's quote was "Thoughts of great deeds are mine." The boys focused on hair, Marcella on ambition.

Elsewhere in *The Scrip*, the Soldan yearbook, I found a page called "The Line-Up," which listed each student's name, favorite saying, hobby, hangout, and greatest desire. Marcella's favorite saying was "Well, listen here!" Below her, Myra Latta's favorite saying was "Oh, giggle," while Jane Newman liked to say, "That's the cutest thing I ever saw!" Marcella's hobbies were "arguing." Other students' hobbies included "wearing short sleeves" and "chewing gum" and "talking baby talk." The greatest desires from her classmates were "to jump rope," "to be married," "to be attractive," "to vamp the boys." Marcella's greatest desire? "To ride in an aeroplane." It was clear that she was unique.

In contrast to her sister, Ruth went to Central High School, a large public school in St. Louis. She also stood out on her page of the 1921–1922 *Red and Black* with the quote under her senior photo: "Thought is deeper than all speech, Feeling deeper than all thought." Take that, Joseph Reeves, a fellow student who was super psyched to be "as true as steel, a friend indeed." Ruth also had written a short story that was published in her yearbook. It was called "Halfway to Heaven," and it was about a little girl who loved the sunset. Whenever she was playing, she would stop at the sight of a sunset.

She loved the colors . . . the yellows and mauves and pinks
and violets that glowed for a space in pastel loveliness; she

EDWARD HAVERSTICK

"Thine was the sunniest
nature
That ever drew the air."

Class Play
Nifty Fifty, '18, '19
'20, '21, '22

ROSE MINKOWITZ

"Times of joy and times
of woe,
Each an angel-presence
know.".

Girls' Literary, '21, '22
La Castilla, '21
Commercial Club, '21, '22
Greek Games, '19

ISADORE GOLDENBERG

"Moderation, the noblest
gift of heaven."

JOSEPH REEVES

"As true as steel, a friend
indeed."

Class Play
Nifty Fifty, '20, '21, '22
President, '22
Student Council, '20, '22
Glee Club
Track, '20, '21, '22

RUTH MORRIS

"Thought is deeper than
all speech,
Feeling deeper than all
thought."

Declamatory Contest, '20
Red and Black, '21

LLOYD BEAN

"But a merrier man,
Within the limits of be-
coming mirth
I never spent an hour's
talk withal."

French Club
Class Play

Ruth Morris's yearbook, 1922

loved the images she could make out in the clouds in the
sunset. For she saw in it wonderful sights—Carthage on
her golden river, houses and castles all purple, with orange spires; Fujiyama's great purple bulk with flashing
golden-white summit rising from a shimmering sea of
gold and orange; the flaming Amazon flowing through
purple tropical forests through which brilliant crimson-
plumaged birds darted; all this and more she saw in the
sunset, and she loved—loved till her inner most being
ached from surfeit of loving.

The girl in the story lived across the street from an "old, old-
fashioned building that the Board of Education was always meaning to tear down but never did." The building had not many
windows but a huge tower rising three or four stories into the air,
and the child imagined that if she could see such beautiful sunsets
from the ground, imagine what she could see from a tower that
"reaches halfway to heaven." The little girl plots and plans, and one
day when no one is around, she slips into the unlocked school and
begins her ascent to the "huge, gloomy garret" with "deep, impen-
etrable shadows in the corners." And though she was afraid, she
kept on going. Up flights of steps to rickety ladders she climbed,
remembering how a very daring boy had tried to climb up to the
top of the tower but came back, his face pale because the ladders
and floors were rotted out and they wouldn't hold his weight. Although the little girl was very afraid, she kept going up, and "what

waited for her at the top gave her courage." More climbing, more floors, more rickety ladders, and finally she reached the last one. "With courage that many men might envy, she climbed up and it was underneath a trap door." The little girl confidently put her hand on the latch but the trapdoor wouldn't open. She whimpered and looked down and could see nothing but darkness. She felt dizzy and faint and "for very weakness, she almost let go." Then one of her little hands found a latch and creakily but easily the door slid open, and she climbed up and stood on the tiny platform that was the highest in the city. Then she lifted her eyes above her.

From a Vesuvius, all smoldering red and gray, as large as one third of the universe, rose the shape of an angel, and it filled the remainder of the universe. A mighty, magnificent woman-shape, purple, with burnished outspread wings, and golden rays crowning the head. Great, protecting arms were stretched down to the little girl and a face, in shadow with features scarcely discernible, yet holding the mother-look was bent over the child. And the child stood, motionless and adoring, staring at the divine figure.

If you had been watching from below, you could have seen, at the very top of that tower, a tiny black speck against the colors of the sunset sky, a speck that was a human child silhouette, lifeless as a statue, with head thrown back and arms raised to heaven.

And the child said, "Because I have come such a long and difficult way, God has let me see one of His visions"; and she stood thus, until the figure melted into the gray of twilight and the twilight into the darkness and the stars came out. Then she dropped her hands to her side and climbed down from the little platform. Then she went down all those ladders though all was black and only by feeling could she find her way. And though at the bottom of each ladder her foot waved in a black void that might be all eternity before it found a place to rest, she yet was not afraid, because in the sky above her, unseen in the night, was still that mother-angel that watched over her. She made her way down to the garret floor, and then she walked down the long stairs, and out into the early evening street where the lights were lit. And she never told anyone of her ascent halfway to heaven, until now.

This heartbreaking story was written by a seventeen-year-old motherless girl.

Reading of Ruth's longing for her mother moved me so much. As a child, I was very attached to my own mother (and to be honest, as an adult I'm really attached to her as well), and I can't fathom what my life would have been like if I'd lost her when I was as young as Ruth. So much of my stability and confidence came from her steadfast support.

What had happened to Ruth's mother? I had still not been able to locate a death certificate for Clara.

Weeks later, as I was looking for something else online, I came across a strange piece of information. A Clara Morris who very much sounded like the Morris sisters' mother was listed in the census records for 1920, 1930, and 1940, but this Clara Morris's address was 5400 Arsenal Road in St. Louis. When I searched that address, what came up was even more perplexing: the history page of the Missouri Department of Mental Health.

I discovered that in 1910, 5400 Arsenal Road was the address of the St. Louis Insane Asylum, formerly the St. Louis County Lunatic Asylum (it was later called the City Sanitarium, then Missouri State Hospital, and now St. Louis Psychiatric Rehabilitation Center).

I ordered a copy of the 1953 death certificate for the Clara Morris at this address, and when it came my suspicion was confirmed: This was the Morris sisters' mother. Guerson Morris was listed as her husband and her address as the insane asylum at 5400 Arsenal Road. She arrived there sometime between 1910 and 1920 and was there until she died in 1953. She had lived there for more than thirty years.

To say I was surprised by this new information would be an understatement. I was stunned. This wasn't any part of the Morris sisters' lives that I knew. We had always been told that Clara had died while giving birth to Ruth.

I needed to talk to Claire.

FIVE

Remembering Mama

When I called Claire in the Keys, I could hear the tropical birds chattering in the background.

"So, I decided to write about the Morris sisters," I began.

"Finally!" she said.

"Claire, I've started doing some preliminary research and I don't think their mother died in St. Louis. I mean, she did die in St. Louis, but not from tuberculosis or in childbirth."

"I know," Claire said quietly.

"You do?" This was a surprise.

"Jule, it was a very different time. It's not like now."

I wanted to make sure I understood what Claire was saying. "So you knew that she was in a mental institution," I said.

Claire paused. "You want to hear the real true story of the Morris sisters?"

"Yes, please."

"Okay. So this is the real true story of the Morris sisters," she began, and I started writing.

"The family lived in Montreal," Claire explained. Canada was where all of my grandmother's family emigrated from after leaving Romania in the late nineteenth century (I knew about our Canadian relatives from my grandmother as well), and before moving on to New York, but actually I had never found a record of the Morrises in Canada. It was possible that Claire might be wrong on some details—but not, I hoped, the larger story.

"The father was a violinist. He was asked to join the St. Louis Philharmonic. He took his wife, three daughters, and a son—packed everything and went to St. Louis by train.

"Selma was the oldest, Sam next, then Malvina and then Marcella. The mother, who was your great-grandmother Martha's sister, became pregnant again in St. Louis. There she had Ruth. She must have had that post-pregnancy depression and in those years they had no psychiatrists or drugs for that, so they put her in an institution for the insane."

I took notes as Claire continued. "The father couldn't handle the kids, so he put them in the Hebrew Orphan Asylum. After a while he left St. Louis and his family. The children were brought up as orphans in the home. They went to school and as Selma told me many times, they got a great business education.

"If it was today they would give the mother a pill and she would be fine. My mother said Clara and her sisters—one of whom was your great-grandmother—were the most beautiful girls. They were very sought after."

I remember that my grandmother used to tell us that when she was a girl, her mother would take off for weeks or even months, leaving my grandmother, her sister, and four brothers with her father, who was a dress designer. She always referred to her mother as "strong and independent." Later my mother always said, "What's strong about leaving your kids?" Listening to Claire, I began to wonder if, like her sister, my great-grandmother had some kind of mental illness. Claire thought Clara had been depressed, but she didn't really know, of course, and there was a good chance that in 1910 doctors didn't really know either—even doctors at the asylum.

I couldn't help but wonder if the catalyst for taking the mother of five children out of her home and placing her in an insane asylum would have to be something dramatic.

I needed to find out what had happened to Clara, so I reached out to the Missouri Department of Mental Health. My request was simple:

To Whom It May Concern:

I am currently writing a book about my great-aunts. They emigrated from Romania to St. Louis in 1902 when their mother gave birth to her fifth child. They told people she had died in childbirth, but she was actually placed in the St. Louis Lunatic Asylum (her address on census records was 5400 Arsenal Road) from approximately 1910–1953, and her children were placed in a Jewish orphanage in St. Louis. I am wondering if there is any way I can speak to someone about her, or gain access to her records. Her name was Clara Morris, she was born in 1876.

I sent an email explaining who I was and what I was looking for.

A reply came within a few days.

Hi Julie,

We would love to help, however you are looking for the St. Louis Psychiatric Rehabilitation center or the Dome building.

I am trying to think of who I should direct you to there, but may need to ask around a bit. I was actually just there yesterday for a meeting with the Regional Director for the hospital. I will send him an email and find out what I can for you.

Elizabeth

In the meantime, I wrote to the hospital directly and asked if I could have access to Clara's records. I was told that for legal reasons I could not.

I wrote to Elizabeth again.

Hi Elizabeth,

I got an email back that I won't be able to get to the records of my great-great-aunt without a court order because of a HIPAA law. I am going to get a lawyer to try and do it. I wonder if you know anything about this or can suggest someone there who might know. I called the [Missouri] Supreme Court and they weren't sure either, but the person I talked to thought the

records might be at the Department of Mental Health
in Jefferson City (but I think he was guessing).

Thanks so much for any guidance you might be able to
give me.

Best,
Julie

Hi Julie,

I'm really sorry to hear that! I was hoping that connection would
work out.

I don't know much about obtaining records, unfortunately.
Nor do I have any legal resources I could direct to you. I wish I
could.

I will add a bit of optimism in saying that I think you have a
good chance of reaching your goal once you acquire a lawyer
who can navigate the legal speak.

I am getting ready to travel for the next week, and won't be
available via email or phone. But if you send me a reminder on
the 7th, I can do some research locally. Specifically I would call
the contact given and ask about process. They may be more
receptive to me, as a peer and local resident. It's worth a shot.

Either way, best of luck to you, and I hope to hear a success
story about these trials in the near future!

All the best,
Elizabeth

While it was frustrating not being able to gain access to Clara's
records, I knew that I was lucky to be looking for this information
in St. Louis and not New York City. Everyone I spoke to or contacted in St. Louis was courteous, helpful, and interested (yay,
Midwest!)—a far cry from the bureaucrats I deal with every day
in New York City.

. . .

I LOOKED INTO St. Louis–based lawyers of all kinds and emailed several of them to see if they could help me, but the few who responded were not at all familiar with this kind of situation and didn't seem eager to learn. I decided to call my cousin Jim, who is the lawyer in my family (as opposed to my cousin Barry, who is the doctor in my family—both on the non-Morris side). Jim said his firm was in a network of lawyers all over the country and that he could get me names of lawyers in St. Louis who might be able to help. Which he did.

Armed with this list, I called the first lawyer and actually managed to get him on the phone. He found the story of the Morris sisters intriguing (at least my telling of it), though he admitted that he had no idea about the laws surrounding access to records. But unlike the other lawyers I'd been in touch with so far, he wanted to research what was possible and get back to me. He said he wanted to figure out a way to get the records without having to petition the court, because there was no guarantee that a judge would even grant the order. It was a week later when he sent a letter to the St. Louis Psychiatric Rehabilitation Center on what looked to me like fancy lawyer stationery. It said:

I represent Julie Klam. Ms. Klam has discovered that one of her ancestors, Clara Schneirer Morris, was committed to the Arsenal Street Hospital around 1910 and lived there until her death in 1953. Julie Klam has confirmed Mrs. Morris' presence there in every decennial census from 1910–1940.

She inquired with you earlier about getting Mrs. Morris' records from your archives and was told she would need a court order. Our research on this matter indicates that HIPAA protection for medical records only lasts 50 years. The 50 year requirement in the case of Clara Schneirer Morris ended in 2003. Please provide medical records and the file from Clara Schneirer Morris from the date of her admission to her death.

I was over the moon. I felt like finding out what happened to Clara would start me on the road to finding the answers to so many questions about the Morris sisters.

A few days later, the lawyer's assistant called me. The St. Louis Psychiatric Rehabilitation Center had called my lawyer and told him it would agree to release Clara Morris's records, but there had been a flood in the basement of the Arsenal Street building many years ago that destroyed decades of records, so they didn't have much.

I couldn't believe it. An act of God was going to keep me from finding out what happened to the Morris sisters' mother.

SIX

Start at the Very Beginning, a Very Good Place to Start

I decided to go to St. Louis and visit the flooded basement and look myself to see what I could find. It wasn't a rational decision, but I couldn't help but feel that nobody had really paid attention to the Morris sisters and their parents—both in my own family and in the world—and that these women deserved the attention and any effort I could make on their behalf. I was starting to feel like their surrogate.

A few days later an envelope arrived from the Missouri Department of Mental Health. Inside was a cover letter typed all in capital letters that said (using a lot of legalese) that the information it was providing me was not to be used to criminally investigate or prosecute any drug or alcohol abuse client. Fair enough.

Also included were two photocopies. The first was an index card. In its entirety it said:

No: 1139 FORM 89-M

Name: MORRIS, Clara

Address: 1449 Cass

Date of Birth: 11-17-1875   Color: W   Sex: F

Admitted: 9-20-1910   Discharged: 12-29-1953

Relative's Name: Thelma Morris, Dtr. 7129 Dartmouth, St. Louis

Remarks: Schiz.

The second page was a black background with white letters that said:

NAME: Morris, Clara   COM: 176 CASE #11339

ADDRESS: 1449 Cas   ADMITTED: 9/20/1910

BIRTHPLACE: Romania   D.O.B.: 11/17/1875

ADMITTED FROM: City Hospital

SEX: F   COLOR: W   AGE: 35   DIAGNOSIS: Schiz; Senility

MARITAL STATUS: Widow   NO. OF CHILDREN: 5

OCCUPATION: Housework   DATE OF DEPARTURE:
12/29/1953

FATHER: John Bleck   BIRTHPLACE: Russia   RESULT: Died

MOTHER: Goy Dietack   BIRTHPLACE: Austria

CAUSE OF DEATH: Cerebro-vascular emboli with rt heriplegia,
Multiple emboli terminal

NAME OF RELATIVES	RELATIONSHIP	ADDRESS
G. B. Morris	Husband	1449 Cass
Selma Morris	Daughter	6301 Delmar
Malvina Morris	Daughter	257 W 4th St. NY City

So there it was in actual black and white. Clara Morris had been admitted to a mental hospital in St. Louis in 1910 when Ruth was six years old and Selma was seventeen. It wasn't just the stress of having a new baby in the family or even postpartum depression that she suffered from: It was schizophrenia, which in 1910 could easily have been a misdiagnosis. She was committed when William Howard Taft was president and before women had the right to vote, and she never left, dying in the asylum forty-three years later when Dwight D. Eisenhower was president and *I Love Lucy* was the most popular show on television—a household gadget that wasn't even invented when she was on the outside.

Reading copies of these files, so direct and cold and unfeeling—so *official*—I felt a deep and profound sadness for Clara and her children. What they must have suffered, I couldn't even begin to imagine.

I did some research into the treatment of psychiatric patients in 1910, and what I found was just as shocking. Treatment for patients with the issues Clara confronted consisted of a patient getting either a lot of fresh air or untested, barbaric physical treatments.

I was even more committed to going to St. Louis. I knew the asylum was now just an empty building, but it was still standing, and I kept thinking that maybe there might be some clues about Clara or her family—something that might give me insight into their lives. If nothing else, I would be able to pay my respects. I was pretty sure no one in our family had been there before.

AT THE SAME TIME I was investigating Clara, I was also trying to locate any records from the Jewish orphanage where the Morris sisters had been placed. I didn't know which orphanage they were in—there were several in St. Louis at the time—so I decided to investigate all of them until I found the right one. I came across Viki Fagyal, a volunteer and officer at the St. Louis Genealogical Society, who had written extensively about the history of orphanages in St. Louis. I emailed her and asked if we could set up a phone call. She agreed.

She told me that in her experience, it was virtually impossible for people to get any records from the Jewish orphanages in St. Louis, because you had to go through the Jewish Board of Family and Children's Services, a national organization, and the people there were not at all forthcoming unless you were asking for your own records. She suggested I write to the archivist at the St. Louis Jewish Community Archives, for guidance. Which I did.

I am an author currently working on my sixth book about some relatives of mine who were in a Jewish orphanage in St. Louis sometime in the early 1900s.

Their parents took them from Romania in 1902 and soon after arriving in St. Louis, their mother was committed to the insane asylum and the five children were put in an orphanage.

I am in New York but going to St. Louis in October to research, is this something your records might contain, or without knowing where they were am I looking at a needle in a haystack situation?

Many thanks for your help,
Julie Klam

She wrote back:

Good morning. Interesting research.

The problem with the Jewish orphanages here in St. Louis is that there were many. The actual records of the orphanages are held by Jewish Family & Children's Service, which does not allow access to the records unless you are the person in the records—believe me, several people, including me, have tried.

That said, I do have the minutes of the Jewish Shelter Home/Jewish Home for Children, 1910–1926, which sometimes mentions children (often without last names) as well as the

Dorothy Drey Shelter Home for 1926–1930. There is also the Jewish Shelter Home Board minutes for 1909–1916, but that is usually protocol discussions rather than information about or names of children.

Do you know the name of the institution in which your relatives were housed?

While this was a step in the right direction, it wasn't a great leap forward.

Thanks so much for getting back to me. I don't know the name of the institution, none of the children ever got married or had kids and the people who remember them now don't remember much else. I would be very interested in anything you have, though it's seeming more likely that I won't find actual records but may at least be able to get a sense of what life was like.

From the archivist:

Hmm. I also have some information about the other orphanages in the community. If you have some names (and dates of when here), I'd be happy to do a cursory check before you head this way.

Not sure when in October you are heading this way, but the Archives (actually all entities in the community) will be closed for much of October because of the Jewish Holidays.

There are other places in St. Louis, such as the Missouri History Museum, that also might be able to assist you. I'd be happy to chat with you about that also.

Me:

My October trip was sort of arbitrarily chosen because I'm going to Romania in December, but I can definitely change it to later (November?) if more facilities are open. (Also, my boyfriend is from Iowa and he said to get there before weather becomes an issue with flights.)

The names of the children are:

Samuel Morris b. 1897
Selma Morris b. 1893
Malvina Morris b. 1899
Marcella Morris b. 1901
Ruth Morris b. 1904

They are listed as living at home in the 1910 census so it would have been probably very close to 1911–1915.

I am very interested in the Missouri History Museum (there is also a historical society I believe?).

Thank you again so much!

From the archivist:

I'll run these names and let you know if we have anything that can help immediately. You might indeed want to change your date of coming this way because of the holidays. November is usually OK here in terms of weather.

The Missouri History Museum is indeed the historical society. They were originally the society, then changed to the museum, and are now trying to decide if they want to return to society. Whew!

They do have a good online presence (website under library & research center, under search the collections, then genealogy index). Although that is by no means all they have, it is a good way to get started. Their archives are excellent and they have a card catalog that defies description in that it is a card index of things in the library. And they have the city directories—hard copy! Wonderful stuff.

I'll check these names in my indices and let you know what I find.

Me:

Oh fantastic and wow! I will go to their website right now and in the meantime plan my trip for November!

Thanks a million!

I realized I was starting to develop relationships with people based on their enthusiasm for my project (and their kindness), and I was feeling less alone and daunted. I wished the Morris sisters had had this kind of help.

I knew it was probable that the Morris children were out of the orphanage by 1920, as all of them would have been sixteen or older by then, and the likelihood was very low that all of the kids had been in the one orphanage that she had the minutes for and that they'd be mentioned in them. I was discovering on my own something that I later realized all genealogists know: The experience of tracking down leads is like working for weeks and weeks to figure out how to get a locked door to open. You do everything you can, banging and tinkering with the lock, and finally you pick up a key you never thought would work and the door magically opens. And then you find there's a cement wall behind it. You might take a chisel to the wall for a while, a few promising chunks fall out, but at some point you think, "I'm going to get through this cement wall and find a steel door." Then you wonder whether you should look for a completely different door or just keep trying to figure out a way through this one. There were so many gaping holes in my knowledge of the Morris sisters, and I was very realistically afraid that some of them might remain that way.

In my discouragement, I took a break from research and did something I knew I could accomplish: I booked two trips, one to St. Louis for November and another to Romania for December. If searching wasn't uncovering what I wanted to know about the Morrises while I sat in New York, at least I could visit the places the family had lived and maybe glean something from them.

During this time, I was having lunch with my "aunt" Alex (she had been married to my parents' best friend until he passed away in 1991). Her father was the famous magazine editor and writer Herbert Mayes. I explained the problems I was having finding the truth about what happened to the Morris sisters. She told me that her father had written the definitive biography of Horatio Alger, except it was all made up. It was called *Alger: A Biography without a Hero* and was published in 1928. She said her father had started to research Alger and found that the facts about him were either boring or impossible to find, so he decided just to write the book, making most of it up. Then when it was published, what he had made up was taken as fact, and he just went along with it. The Horatio Alger Society nominated him as a member and declared his book to be required reading for all Horatio Alger fans. It's still listed on the Horatio Alger Society's book list, but the society now admits, "Up until 1961, this completely fictitious account of Alger's life was the only biography of Alger ever written. The book recounts a version of Alger's life based on a diary and letters that never existed. For nearly forty years, this biography was accepted as definitive and accurate, and even today it is still mistakenly cited as a reliable source in most reference texts. In the author's own words, this version of Alger's life 'literally swarms . . . with countless absurdities.'"

I laughed and Alex said, "Of course I'm not suggesting you make anything up, but it worked for him for thirty-three years."

Reader, I have made nothing up, but I know exactly how Alex's father, Mr. Mayes, felt.

I TALKED TO several historians and historical novelists about how they track down facts that are difficult to find. One historical novelist explained that most of the people she writes about are famous enough that there is a lot of research available and in a variety of sources: books, archives, museums. But sometimes the details or background you're looking for are just not to be found. She told me about a time when she was desperately trying to locate a particular gravestone in a vast cemetery. She searched the cemetery for hours and finally stopped, tired and discouraged. She took a deep breath and asked the universe for help. She continued walking and suddenly saw a bright red cardinal land on a gravestone. She walked over to it and lo and behold, it was the gravestone she was looking for.

"Sometimes you ask for help and it comes and you don't know why or where it's come from," she told me. "You just accept it and give thanks."

I thought at the very least I'd have a chance of spotting a cardinal or two in St. Louis.

SEVEN

Small Medium at Large

I kept thinking that if only I could just talk to the Morris sisters, all of my questions would be answered. And I've always believed that there's more to life than what we see. Given those two beliefs, I decided to explore an unconventional research avenue and consult a medium. I hoped that it might be my version of asking the universe for help.

I have consulted with psychics and mediums and astrologers many times before, especially when I was in my twenties, so it wasn't a totally foreign idea to me, though every person I asked for a psychic recommendation made some lame joke about the absurdity. (I gently hexed them.)

A friend who'd written a book about ghosts suggested that I

contact Lily Dale Assembly, which is a community in upstate New York that consists entirely of spiritual mediums. The place calls itself "the World's Largest Center for the Religion of Spiritualism." Spiritualism is a belief that is based on the communication with the dead. It was hugely popular in the Victorian era—even Mary Todd Lincoln practiced spiritualism in the White House. Many of the stories you read about spiritualists are that they are charlatans looking to make money off desperate, grieving people, but there are as many who truly believe certain people have a gift for communicating with the great beyond.

The Lily Dale community has a website with listings of its mediums. The site suggests looking through the list and seeing whom you are drawn to in order to determine which medium to make an appointment with. I spent several days staring at the names as I tried to keep a very open mind. I had to admit I was drawn to none of them. I don't know why, but looking at mediums' websites doesn't give me a spiritual zap. Also a lot of them looked like the old AOL web pages, and while I know that shouldn't have counted against them, it somehow did. (Maybe it should have been the opposite, that their communication was so otherworldly that they didn't bother with updated mortal technology.)

I called my friend Patty, an author who writes about a lot of unusual topics, for help. She remembered that she had read an article about a medium who sounded really good. The writer's husband had died, and when the writer called to make the appointment to consult the medium, the husband started talking to the writer through the medium. And the information was verifiable and, in Patty's and my opinion, miraculous.

I read the piece and tracked down the medium to make an appointment with her, explaining what I was looking for.

"Contacting dead people is not like calling someone on the phone, you know," she said. "I mean I can request people, but it doesn't mean they'll show up. Someone will come, but it may not be these sisters."

At this point I was willing to take my chances, mainly because I had nothing to lose but four hundred bucks, and maybe there was some spirit out there who would offer me a key that would open a door into a room that had not been filled with bricks.

I wanted to talk with the medium before my trips to St. Louis and Romania, in case she had any addresses for me (how adorably optimistic I was), so we made the appointment for the upcoming Sunday evening. Several days before the call, I Googled her so I could have an image of her. She looked like she was in her forties, short, dark hair and a nice smile. She was located in New York City, as was I, but she only conducted appointments on the phone. On Sunday evening I sat down with a legal pad and pen and called her.

She was ready for me. She said there were "people" there with her, and she named some names, but none that I knew. Then my aunt Susie popped in. Susie was my dad's only sister. She was fifteen years younger than him. In 2000, she was diagnosed with ALS, Lou Gehrig's disease, the same disease that took her mother, my grandma Billie, in 1983. Susie died in 2004 at age fifty-five. The words really sounded like her, and I was very happy to hear from her. I told her I loved her and missed her. I wondered if I should tell her how everyone was doing, but then figured she knew already. I asked her if she had ever bumped into the Morris sisters, because I was writing a book about them.

The medium went quiet for about thirty seconds.

"Getting someone, it might be one of them," the medium said. She sounded as if she had her eyes closed.

I was quiet.

"Margaret?" the medium asked.

"Marcella?" I said.

She didn't respond. I was hopeful and anxious.

"Hmm," she said, "they're saying that . . . they are glad you are writing this book."

"Oh great!" I wasn't sure who "they" were, but any of them being there was good news.

She spoke slowly. "They said please don't make it like *Grey Gardens*."

It was funny, I had been thinking a lot about the 1975 documentary since I'd started researching the Morris sisters. Grey Gardens was the name of the decrepit home in East Hampton, New York, where Jackie Kennedy Onassis's relatives Edie Bouvier Beale and her mother, Edith, had lived. Albert and David Maysles made a documentary about them called *Grey Gardens*, where they told the story of their lives. The Beales' was a story of riches to rags, and they were truly eccentric and unconventional. The house was not far from where the Morris sisters lived in Southampton at the same time the Beales lived there.

"Okay," I said, "like how do they mean?"

"Something . . . people will laugh at," the medium said firmly. And then she paused to listen again, adding, "She's talking . . ."

I waited. This was what I was hoping for.

"You have to understand that we loved each other very much," the medium said. "We were very close and loving and cared for each other. We only had each other and we were very devoted, and we really, really loved each other."

It wasn't the illuminating insight or long-hidden clue I'd been hoping for, such as the location of an antique trunk filled with a trove of diaries the sisters had kept over the years and photos and clothes and documents. But later, after I'd had a chance to think over what the medium had told me, the more I thought that if I were dead and communicating with a descendant of mine who was writing about me, the one request I'd probably make is "Don't make me into a joke." The fact is, the Morris sisters' attributed quirkiness was a big part of what attracted me to their story and what I thought made it interesting: Everything I had heard about them over the years was framed in that context. So here one of them—though I don't know which one—was asking me not to make them look foolish. Whether or not it was really them, I couldn't help feeling the request was kind of brilliant. And very human.

The only other detail the sisters passed on to me through the medium—and I was more and more certain that it was the Morris sisters—was that they were sorry to hear that Carnegie Deli was closing.

I said I was, too.

EIGHT

Meet Me in St. Louis, Louis

I can't really explain why I felt so strongly that I should visit every place the Morris family lived, but I did. It might have been because I always have a very strong sense of place. Would I be able to feel something if I walked where Clara and Guerson had walked, or seen where the sisters grew up or even played? Maybe some insight or truth about them might hit me and I'd start to understand a bit more about them and their lives. That was my hope, anyway. At the very least, it was a tangible activity, an *action*, and I really needed to feel that I was doing something. Plus it seemed really interesting.

I knew that all of the Morris family came from Romania, and that they came from the part of the country that was closer to Moldova than Transylvania (which was a little disappointing because

I wanted to visit Dracula's castle). Before I went, though, I wanted to make sure the Morrises really came from there and that there was a town or something remaining to visit. It turns out if you Google "Romanian birth records from the nineteenth century," you get a bold message that says there is no central office for vital records in Romania. And if you want copies of birth, marriage, divorce, or death records, you have to write to the Civil Registration District Office in the town hall where the birth, death, or marriage occurred (and it's best to write the request in Romanian).

Birth certificates from that era were handwritten in Romanian, and most of them are still located in physical file cabinets in the original places where the births were registered, guarded by bureaucratic golems. In other words, sitting in my apartment in New York, I was not going to be able to get the Romanian birth certificates myself. I needed help.

Before I left, I contacted the Romanian Genealogical Society in Mendota Heights, Minnesota. (The Midwest is a hotbed of genealogy!) I was directed to an expert genealogist in Romania named Dr. Ladislau Gyémánt, an author and a professor of Jewish history at a university in Cluj, a city in northwest Romania near Transylvania. I emailed him and told him I was looking for any documents—birth, marriage, land deeds, death certificates—relating to the Morris family. I told him I had come across the names of two towns in documents I'd found—Focșani and Râmnicu Sărat.

Dr. Gyémánt replied to say he could help me. He would charge me for his work (finding and translating any vital records) as well as his travel and accommodations, which he said would cost around $150 for two nights. However, at the moment he was teaching, so he wouldn't be able to make the trip from Cluj to Focșani (which was about an eight-hour drive) for another six weeks or so.

I was thrilled, and encouraged. He seemed to know what he was doing, and I had no doubt we would find out a great deal about the early parts of the Morris sisters' lives.

In the meantime, I firmed up plans to go to St. Louis. I told my friend Barbara that I was going to track down what happened to some relatives of mine (I had been trying to make it sound like an Indiana Jones adventure). She said it sounded like fun and asked if she could come with me. She had moved out of New York City to New Hampshire several years ago, so we didn't get to see each other enough. I was grateful for the company.

WHY THE MORRISES ended up in St. Louis was among the early and trickier questions I tried to answer. There was the family story of them getting marooned there on the way to Los Angeles, but I knew now that it wasn't true. When I found the SS *Kensington*'s manifest, the answer to the question "Whether going to join a relative and if so, what relative, their name and address" read "C. Morris, 1100 23rd Street, St. Louis, Mo." Bernhard, Clara, and Sali had St. Louis as a destination in mind even before they left Europe, most likely when they decided to come.

I wasn't sure if "Sali" was Selma or Sam, but clearly the sisters weren't listed with them, though I had no doubt that they came together.

I had a few addresses in St. Louis that I wanted to visit: their first home from the census, the asylum where Clara was committed, and now this C. Morris. I was sure I would find more when I got there.

Before I left I made appointments to meet Viki Fagyal of the St. Louis Genealogical Society and emailed Larry Harmon, an amateur historian who worked at the Missouri Institute of Mental Health, about giving us a tour of the Dome, the former insane asylum.

The day before Barbara and I were to leave, I got an email from the archivist at the St. Louis Jewish Community Archives:

Well, well, well. I found them—at least I found Ruth, Marcella and Malvina. The other two, Samuel & Selma, are not listed in the minutes I have. It appears that Ruth & Marcella entered the Jewish Shelter Home Nov. 25, 1910 (at least they are mentioned in the minutes for that date on p.1).

There are actually several entries about Malvina. She entered the home later than Ruth & Marcella, on Feb. 23, 1911 (p.1). They note specifically that she was lame. There are 5 other entries for her 1911 through 1913.

I looked all the way up to 1930, and they weren't mentioned again.

These are just entries in the minutes, not their actual records, which is why I have anything about them at all. I'll see about getting you copies of the pages.

I couldn't believe it. I read the email over and over, each time more excited about what was found. I emailed back a gushing thank you. Getting copies of the minutes was such great news that I did a little dance that I now think of as the Morris Jubilee.

I also heard back from Larry Harmon about setting up a time:

I would love to meet with you and hopefully be able to help. I used to give informal tours of the Dome building of which you speak. My tour was mainly about the architecture, amenities, surrounding area and fun facts. Like just across the street is a crematory and columbarium where Frank James, the brother of the infamous Jesse James, was cremated and kept. I mentioned little about the specific treatment of patients as I found most people were interested in the other facts. We would go from the very bottom basement where the "worst" patients were kept, to the tip top inside the dome. I still have my notes from when those tours were given including photographs of various documents.

Attached is a photo of a document stating reasons one might be admitted to the hospital. The other attachment is a photo of what the hospital would have looked like in 1910. It had just been expanded to accommodate 2000 patients and 300 employees. This facility was constantly over populated. I believe that I can get us in for a tour if you are interested.

If you are interested more in the history of specific treatment of patients, I may be able to set up a meeting with the COO of the current St. Louis Psychiatric Rehab Center during your time here in St. Louis.

The Dome building is in an historic neighborhood called The Hill. As the name suggests, it is built on the highest elevation in St. Louis and is famous for a traditional collection of authentic Italian bakeries, grocery stores, restaurants and mom-and-pop trattorias. It would be a shame for you to visit the area without eating at one of the restaurants. I hope you like Italian food!

I wrote to Barbara about the plans and also included the attachment Larry Harmon had sent me called "Reasons of Admission 1864 to 1889," which listed reasons why people were admitted to an insane asylum. (It turned out to be compiled from the logbook of the West Virginia Hospital for the Insane.)

"Okay, I'm in for the first item on the list," Barbara said.

"Yes," I said, "put me down for the third."

"Wait," she said, "'marriage of a son'? 'Gathering in the head'?"

"Hmm," I said, "is wearing a tampon 'suppression of menses'?"

"Oy."

"Do you get more points if you have more than one?" I asked.

"Yes. It's sergeant's stripes or teardrop tattoos," she said.

"Why is 'shooting of daughter' a whole category?" I asked, and then said, "Ooh, 'dropsy.' My kid has that."

"'Bad company'! You could be committed for being in the seventies band?"

"'Uterine derangement' sounds very messy!"

"And 'fell from a horse in war,' not just any fall from a horse."

"Yeah, unless there's a war, you're just clumsy. 'Rumor of husband murder' seems constitutionally sound."

ONCE I HAD the list and did more research on it, I saw that a lot of people were making jokes about it, as we had, and then I realized: This list of reasons was the extent of the knowledge of psychology

REASONS FOR ADMISSION
1864 TO 1889

INTEMPERANCE & BUSINESS TROUBLE	DISSOLUTE HABITS
KICKED IN THE HEAD BY A HORSE	DOMESTIC AFFLICTION
HEREDITARY PREDISPOSITION	DOMESTIC TROUBLE
ILL TREATMENT BY HUSBAND	DROPSY
IMAGINARY FEMALE TROUBLE	EGOTISM
HYSTERIA	EPILEPTIC FITS
IMMORAL LIFE	EXCESSIVE SEXUAL ABUSE
IMPRISONMENT	EXCITEMENT AS OFFICER
JEALOUSY AND RELIGION	EXPOSURE AND HEREDITARY
LAZINESS	EXPOSURE AND QUACKERY
MARRIAGE OF SON	EXPOSURE IN ARMY
MASTURBATION & SYPHILIS	FEVER AND JEALOUSY
MASTURBATION FOR 30 YEARS	FIGHTING FIRE
MEDICINE TO PREVENT CONCEPTION	SUPPRESSED MASTURBATION
MENSTRUAL DERANGED	SUPPRESSION OF MENSES
MENTAL EXCITEMENT	THE WAR
NOVEL READING	TIME OF LIFE
NYMPHOMANIA	UTERINE DERANGEMENT
OPIUM HABIT	VENEREAL EXCESSES
OVER ACTION OF THE MIND	VICIOUS VICES
OVER STUDY OF RELIGION	WOMEN TROUBLE
OVER TAXING MENTAL POWERS	SUPERSTITION
PARENTS WERE COUSINS	SHOOTING OF DAUGHTER
PERIODICAL FITS.	SMALL POX
TOBACCO & MASTURBATION	SNUFF EATING FOR 2 YEARS
POLITICAL EXCITEMENT	SPINAL IRRITATION
POLITICS	GATHERING IN THE HEAD
RELIGIOUS ENTHUSIASM	GREEDINESS
FEVER AND LOSS OF LAW SUIT	GRIEF
FITS AND DESERTION OF HUSBAND	GUNSHOT WOUND
ASTHMA	HARD STUDY
BAD COMPANY	RUMOR OF HUSBAND MURDER
BAD HABITS & POLITICAL EXCITEMENT	SALVATION ARMY
BAD WHISKEY	SCARLATINA
BLOODY FLUX	SEDUCTION & DISAPPOINTMENT
BRAIN FEVER	SELF ABUSE
BUSINESS NERVES	SEXUAL ABUSE & STIMULANTS
CARBONIC ACID GAS	SEXUAL DERANGEMENT
CONGESTION OF BRAIN	FALSE CONFINEMENT
DEATH OF SONS IN WAR	FEEBLENESS OF INTELLECT
DECOYED INTO THE ARMY	FELL FROM HORSE IN WAR
DERANGED MASTURBATION	FEMALE DISEASE
DESERTION BY HUSBAND	DISSIPATION OF NERVES

and mental health at the time. Suddenly it wasn't all that funny anymore.

As someone who has her share of neuroses, I was horrified to think that someone (probably a man) could diagnose another person's (probably a woman's) depression and determine that the reason for institutionalizing her was "novel reading." No wonder the Morris sisters never married: Most of the men they encountered over the course of their lives were disappointing to say the least.

There is a distance that we tend to put between ourselves and the awful things that happened a long time ago—it's history, after all, not life today. But the little details you notice spark your attention, and you realize that the citizens of Pompeii were not cartoon characters or lines in history textbooks. They were real people who lived and loved and suffered and died. I understand it's self-protective to not embrace every horror that has ever happened in the world by processing them today as events that happened a long time ago. After I graduated from college, I spent about a year immersed in the history of the Holocaust: I felt I needed to identify with my people's suffering and also self-flagellate for being privileged and lucky to have been spared such horrors. My father, who grew up during the Depression in Harlem and was beaten up on his way home from school every day, did not understand my fascination. He somewhat angrily challenged me and my obsession. I think he felt that he'd done everything he could to give my brothers and me a lovely, bucolic, and very safe childhood so that those monstrous images could be kept out of my head, so my life would be happier than his. It's this search for a happy life, a good outcome, that defines my father to me. As long as I've known him, he has always only watched movies that he knew had happy endings.

He won't even watch his sports teams play live: He records the games, and if they lose, he won't watch. As I've gotten older, I've come to understand that tendency, that need for good outcomes, but when I was younger I thought he was just out of touch.

Just before we departed, I did receive the scans of the minutes about the Morris sisters in the orphanage:

MINUTES-MEETING SHELTER HOME.

Nov. 25, 1910

Two Morris children (Ruth and Marcella) entered. Father Photographer, and mother in Insane Asylum.

There it was, in black and white.

MINUTES OF MEETING

Feb. 23, 1911

At Columbian Club at 8:15.

Mr. Ittleson occupied the chair, and Mrs. Friedman noted as Secretary.

Minutes read and approved. Mrs. Arnstein Ch. Of Admissions Committee reported that five (5) children were admitted, one (1) removed to C.O.A. The two (2) Levitt children, the children of the cook, Malvina Morris, a lame girl, Mamie Sollenbaum and Sarah Rosen. Names of children entered.

REPORT OF THE JEWISH SHELTER HOME FOR JULY—AUGUST—SEPTEMBER.

Malvina Morris was in the Cripples' Home at Kirkwood during the entire summer. I have asked our secretary to make the proper acknowledgements to these institutions.

Up to September 6th two more children were admitted.

Malvina Morris had returned from Kirkwood, and according to the last list of names submitted to me, there are now thirty-five children in the home.

All admissions were investigated up to September 6th.

MINUTES OF JEWISH SHELTER HOME FOR CHILDREN

May 30th, 1912

Mrs. Goldstein's reports through Mrs. Friedman that:

1. An operation should be performed on Malvina Morris. Secretary asked to write to Dr. Horowitz, the Doctor in charge to ask him to write a letter to the father, stating briefly the need of the operation, so that we may get the father's permission.

MINUTES OF JEWISH SHELTER HOME
FOR CHILDREN

October 31st, 1912

Malvina Morris removed to the Jewish Hospital, where Dr. Hoffman and Dr. Horowitz will operate on her.

MINUTES OF THE JEWISH SHELTER HOME
FOR CHILDREN

February 27th, 1913

Malvina Morris returned to the Home after a 4 month's stay in the hospital.

THINKING ABOUT WHAT these women had been through as children shattered me. Selma was seventeen, and too old to go into the orphanage. Marcella, eight, and Ruth, six, went into the home and a few months later were joined by Malvina. Then Malvina was sent to a "cripples home" and then to a hospital—by herself—for four months, before returning to her sisters in the orphanage.

I had so many questions and was so glad to be heading to where I prayed I'd find answers.

NINE

Needle in a Graveyard

I t was a crisp November morning when Barb and I met at our St. Louis hotel. Sitting in the lobby waiting for her, I saw a woman walk through with four Boston terriers, my favorite breed—one for each Morris sister. I took it as a good omen.

The office of the St. Louis Genealogical Society was located in a business park in a suburb of St. Louis called Maplewood, and when we arrived, Viki Fagyal came out to meet us. She was a warm, affable retiree who seemed to be constantly on the go, searching for answers to people's questions through genealogy. I immediately loved her and hoped we would be friends forever.

The genealogical society was a cluster of rooms and offices, and one large room where volunteers sat at dozens of computers with information from all of the records they were continually uncovering. Viki introduced us and showed us where we could look for information about the Morrises.

Barbara and I sat at a big table and Viki brought us several books that looked like St. Louis phone books, but I wasn't sure what they were.

It felt as if someone had put a body on the table in front of us and said, "This patient needs an appendectomy. Go." Neither one of us knew where to start. Barbara picked a book at random and opened it while I looked over her shoulder. I don't recall what was on the page because the lines of information looked like another language to me.

Viki sensed that we had absolutely no idea what to do or where to start and took pity on us.

"These are cemetery books," she said. "They tell who is buried where. Look for the Morrises!" she directed.

The books were surveys of the St. Louis cemeteries. They weren't just lists of names in alphabetical order. There were maps and descriptions of areas and of course who was buried there. The books had to be regularly updated so it wasn't just a clean, alphabetical list. So we looked for the Morrises. One volume at a time, each of us scanning the names in the books. As the three of us settled in to the job, it suddenly occurred to me that everyone in the cemetery book was dead. Probably even a lot of the people who worked on the cemetery book. So. Many. Dead. People. How were we to find one family in all of these names?

After about a half an hour Viki said, "Found Clara." And a few minutes later, "And Guerson." They were buried in the same cemetery.

She suggested that we should visit the graves. And after that, we should head to the St. Louis Historical Society and Library, where there were more records for us to look through.

I tried to get directions from her but she shook her head. "No. I am taking you."

Her hospitality was an answer to my prayers: Barbara and I were hugely relieved to be getting a local guide. Between the unfamiliar genealogy search and the strange topography of St. Louis—it's not laid out on a grid the way much of New York is, and I don't function well outside of Manhattan—I was kind of like a fish in a little plastic bag. I wasn't going to die, but I wasn't at my best. I was starting to panic that I'd get us hopelessly lost in St. Louis and we would never find anything useful about the Morrises and that our trip would be a complete failure. Viki, once again and not for the last time, saved the day.

WE DROVE TO the New Mount Sinai Cemetery. It is a Jewish cemetery southwest of downtown St. Louis and about a ten-minute drive from the genealogical society office. Viki parked by the door of the cemetery's administration building and took us inside. An attractive woman in a black dress and pearls, her silver hair held in place with a grosgrain hair band, sat behind a desk as if she had been plucked from central casting for "midwestern cemetery receptionist." She smiled at us, conveying kindness and a sense that she was respecting whatever it was that brought us there.

I waited for Viki to say something: It was like when you're a kid and your mother takes you to the doctor's office and you wait for her to tell the person behind the glass window your name and why you're there, and then your mother tells you she wants you to do it. Viki pushed me toward the lady at the desk and said, "Ask your questions."

With my hands dug deep in my pockets, I fumbled out some words that I hoped told the receptionist that we were looking for two gravestones—George or Guerson Morris and Clara Morris.

The woman wasn't the least bit confused or dismissive. In fact, she couldn't have been kinder. She went over to one of many metal file cabinets, this one with the letters *Mo–N* on the tab, and pulled out a manila folder. She found the information she was looking for, wrote down some numbers on a piece of paper, and handed it and several maps of the cemetery to me. She explained that each grave had a tiny number on it so that it could be identified. She showed us where we could find Clara's grave—it was number 580, in section F—and Guerson's number was 1336 in section Q.

I was so excited to have this information, and that I'd (kind of) done it myself. I had the overblown sense of accomplishment my neighbor has when he parallel parks particularly smoothly. We took our maps and confidently headed out through the fall leaves.

Most of the times that I've been to cemeteries I was there for a funeral, and it wasn't hard to figure out where I should go: There was usually a tent over the open grave with chairs around it, a huge mound of dirt and some shovels. But shortly before I went to St. Louis I traveled to Paris with my boyfriend, where we visited both the Père Lachaise Cemetery (where Jim Morrison, Isadora Duncan, and Oscar Wilde are buried) and Montparnasse Cemetery (where Jean-Paul Sartre and Samuel Beckett are buried). I can tell you honestly that despite the very clear maps and many markers to the final resting places of these celebrated artists, some of the graves were impossible to locate: We just couldn't find them.

I don't know why it's so hard to locate specific graves in a cemetery, but a mapping system that makes sense to me seems like the least of a cemetery's priorities.

So Barbara, Viki, and I looked and looked for the graves of Clara and Guerson, and none of us could find them. After a while we split up, each of us taking different sections of the cemetery to look in. The headstones throughout the cemetery were mostly flat in the grass or just small "pillow"-type graves.

FINALLY, AFTER WHAT seemed like hours, Viki called out, "I found her!" Of course it would be Viki.

The gravestone was a small granite rectangle set into the side of a low hill. All that was engraved into the stone was "CLARA MORRIS" and beneath her name "1875–1953."

It was obvious that nobody had visited the grave for quite a while. And even though the cemetery was very well kept, Clara's stone looked as if it had been forgotten—overlooked by those of us still around.

I cleared away the brown leaves, wiped away the dirt that had accumulated on it, and pulled out some weeds that had grown over the edges. I put a stone on the center of the grave and said a prayer to her. Jews put stones on graves for a variety of reasons, because unlike flowers they never die. The Talmud mentions that after a person dies, their soul continues to dwell for a while in the grave where they are buried. Putting stones on a grave keeps the soul down in this world, which some mourners find comforting. Another related interpretation suggests that the stones keep demons and golems from getting into the graves. Also the Hebrew word for pebble is *tz'ror*—and it happens that this word also means "bond." When Jews pray we ask that the deceased be "bound up in the bond of life." By placing a stone on a grave marker, we show that we have been there and that the individual's memory continues to live on in and through us. When my boyfriend and I visited Gertrude Stein's grave in Père Lachaise, it had a tiny pale pebble driveway leading up to it, and people put dark stones on it in the shape of hearts. My mother's sisters' and her parents' graves are crowded with stones. There were none on Clara's, except the one I placed there.

Clara had five children, and none of them had children, so there were no grandchildren or great-grandchildren to visit. Looking around, I couldn't help but see that the entire section of the cemetery felt like that. The newer sections in the distance had graves festooned with flowers, balloons, stuffed animals, and plaques, but those buried in section F seemed to be a bit alone, as if life or the descendants of those buried here had forgotten them.

We left Clara to keep looking for Guerson, but after nearly an hour with no success, we knew we needed help. It wasn't like Jim Morrison's grave where you could follow the crowds.

We went back to the cemetery office and told the woman we just couldn't find the grave for Guerson Morris.

She was stumped. The cemetery's director came out of his office and offered to help. We explained that we'd looked where we'd been directed and we didn't want to say it wasn't there, but . . . He took us back to his office, where there was a wall-size map of the cemetery like the one we were carrying, but on his map you could actually read the numbers. I was impressed.

We showed him where we had been, and he looked at the number again.

"Okay, there's a C next to the number. That would mean it was a child's grave and in a separate section." He looked at us again, his face more somber than it had been. "So this was a child?"

"No," I said, "he was in his seventies."

The director frowned and looked at his map again, and then asked the woman for the file.

She pulled out the original order form and there was a letter attached.

It was typed on onionskin paper, and the top said "29 Charles St. New York City," and it was dated April 12, 1937. It read:

Dear Mr. Mayer:

With reference to the Mt. Sinai Cemetery arrangements for the ashes of my father, we would rather not ask the association to do this without cost, if we can arrange the matter in any other way. May we impose on you just a little further asking that you ascertain how reasonably we can take care of this ourselves? The space required wouldn't be large, and it isn't our intention to put up a marker, but we would prefer to take care of this if we can. Thanking you for your help in this matter, we are very grateful. If you think it would be better that we get in touch with the association, please let us know.

Very truly yours,
Marcella Morris

Beneath that on the same page was a typed note in a darker ink: "Mr. Schlesinger, Please let me know what you can do about this. These people are very poorly, but they are too proud to take this favor without some little compensation." Handwritten on the page was another note that said, "Mayer, cost will be 15 dollars in child's grave leveled," and below that "give him 1336c" and a stamp that read "MAY 4-1937."

Each of us read the letter and looked at each other, not sure what to say. I think the director was trying to be sensitive; these were my relatives after all.

"They weren't poor," I said. I had a flash of a feeling that I was betraying the Morris sisters, and I was instantly sorry I'd said that. Like maybe the director would exhume him and put him in a grown-up grave? I don't know, but more and more I was feeling a deepening responsibility for them.

WE CHECKED THE original order ticket for burial. It said Guerson died of pulmonary tuberculosis at the Jewish Sanatorium at Fee Fee. (Fee Fee was the name of a road where a camp—Camp Fee Fee—was located in St. Louis. It was for Jewish children with tuberculosis.) There was another letter from Marcella that she sent with the fifteen-dollar check, where she thanked Mr. Mayer for his kindness for helping them.

If the Morris sisters hadn't gotten their father a headstone, that would explain why we couldn't find him. But the director looked through their mother Clara's file and found the order for her burial and headstone, and apparently the Morris sisters decided when their mother died to give their father a stone, too.

The cost of burial in 1937 was $15, which translates to around $250 in today's dollars, whereas they paid $200 for their mother's headstone and burial in 1953, which translates to about $2,000 now.

We walked back to the children's section of the cemetery and saw long lines of headstones with dates that were either the same year as the birth or a few years later. As I stood there, I had a feeling that this decision was not made by all four of the sisters and agreed upon.

I came to this conclusion because I know how hard it can be for two or three siblings to agree, and I had the sense that this wasn't a decision that would have been made lightly. I imagined myself in the room with the four of them, and a wave of anxiety went through me.

Not far into the children's graves, nestled among them, was Guerson Morris, whose dates were seventy-two years apart. It was a small rectangle and it said—misspelled—"GERSON B. MORRIS" and underneath it "1865–1937." The sun had shone on Clara's grave when we found it, but Guerson's was dark, and rather than lying flat, it was tilted at an angle, as if it had been lumped in as an afterthought—which it had.

I looked at his stone and thought about the man who was known among his descendants only for abandoning his children. I knew the effect his actions must have had on his children's lives, but standing there, I felt a swell of empathy for him, too. I had no way of knowing what it must have been like to face the future with a wife with mental illness and five children you couldn't support on your own. I knew he never made it to Los Angeles— he never left St. Louis, and whether he wanted to or not, he stayed married to Clara for all of

Guerson and Selma Morris

his life. He must have felt trapped, and maybe putting the children in the orphanage broke his heart. Maybe he really did think he would someday come back for his children and they could resume their lives as a family.

I tried to put a stone on his grave, but it rolled off. I tried several more times, but the stone just wouldn't stay.

THE RECEPTIONIST IN the cemetery office gave us copies of all the paperwork she could about Guerson and Clara, and Barbara, Viki, and I headed to lunch, where we discussed the findings. Clara's burial order included perpetual care, meaning her gravesite receives ongoing repair and general maintenance. Guerson's had none. I took out the folder with the death certificates. Guerson's said that Ruth had been present when Guerson died and listed her address as 237 West Fourth Street in New York City—she wasn't living at Charles Street with Marcella, Malvina, and Selma. It said that Guerson had been born in Romania and that he was married— to Clara. She was still very much alive in the asylum at the time of his death. His occupation was listed as "photographer," and pretty much everything else was what we'd known—though Viki noticed his birth year on the death certificate was listed as 1864. Lord knows if even that was correct.

The original reason I wanted to meet Viki was that she was an expert in orphanages in St. Louis and orphan genealogy. As she drove us around St. Louis, she told me that in the nineteenth century it was common for children who had only one living parent to be placed in an orphanage. They were called "half orphans." There just weren't supports in most places for single parents, unless you had family you could turn to, and many immigrants did not— they were on their own. Which is the situation Guerson faced.

It wasn't until 1909 that there were any child welfare laws in the United States. (Whereas animal cruelty laws had been instituted in the 1860s. In the late nineteenth century, people complained about abuses of children to the ASPCA.)

Viki theorized that we didn't find notes on Selma and Sam Morris in the orphanage files because the two of them would have been too old: Orphanages at the time only admitted children under the age of fourteen. In 1910, when Clara was committed, Sam would have been fourteen and Selma would have been sixteen. I had read about men committing their wives because they wanted to get rid of them, though I didn't believe that was possible in Clara's case. It just didn't make sense to me that Guerson would remove the mother of five children and have to find support for them just because he was tired of her. Also, if Clara had been healthy, Selma would have been able to get her released. I had come to the conclusion that Clara's committal would have been for something dramatic, that she was seriously ill and that her husband and family had neither the skill nor the resources to help her.

Viki agreed and thought there might even be something in the

St. Louis newspapers of the time about what happened to cause her to be committed.

So we headed to the Missouri Historical Library and Archives. It was housed in a beautiful 1927 Byzantine-style former synagogue. Inside there were high vaulted painted ceilings and elegant wood shelves. Research is a much richer experience inside a beautiful, historic place.

We first looked through the library's database at old newspapers from 1910 for any mention of Clara Morris, or an accident or a woman's breakdown in St. Louis. Though we pored over the local papers, we found no mention of Clara or what had happened to her. Her life and her problems seemed to have fallen under the radar.

TEN

Show-Me State of Mind

I hadn't achieved what I'd hoped to on my trip to St. Louis, but Viki really taught me how to do online genealogy research. As I watched her use the library's archives, I saw how she searched for information and details—much differently than I had up to that point. The difference was that she went more methodically and had more patience than I did, and you really can look at any detail as a clue. Also she taught me that there were places to find information that I didn't know existed, even on the Ancestry site—such as in US military records.

Whenever she found a telling detail about the Morris family, I would ask her how she'd found it and she would take me through her steps.

For example, Viki was able to locate the ship's registry for the

SS *Kensington*, the one that listed Bernard, Clara, and Sali (Selma) and didn't include the other three children, though it said "with children [ages] 9/8/10/1." By digging a bit deeper and noticing a tab on the site, Viki found a second page that I had missed, and there they were: Marcella, Malvina, and Sam (Israel). In addition to recording the passengers' names, the manifest asked other questions of the passengers and recorded their answers:

Age (yrs/months)

Married or Single

Calling or Occupation

Able to Read or Write

Nationality

Last Residence

Seaport for Landing in the United States

Final destination in the United States (City, State or town)

Whether Having a ticket to Final Destination

By Whom Was Passage Paid

Whether in Possession of Money, if so, more than $30 and how much if $30 or less

Whether ever been in the United States, and if so when and where

Whether going to join a relative, and if so, what relative, their name and address

Ever in Prison or Almshouse or supported by charity, if yes state which

Whether a Polygamist

Whether under contract, express or implied to labor in the United States,

Condition of Health, Mental or Physical

Deformed or Crippled, nature and cause

Contract ticket number

Number on the list.

After paying for all of their passages to America—a ticket in 1900 cost about thirty dollars—the Morris family landed in New York with a total of five dollars—about one hundred fifty dollars in today's money. But that's getting ahead of things.

The SS *Kensington* docked in New York Harbor and inspectors came on board to check passengers for infectious diseases— cholera, plague, typhoid, measles, and diphtheria, among others. First- and second-class passengers could avoid Ellis Island, but everyone else aboard had to go through there and pass the full inspections. It could take a day for these passengers to even get off the boat.

Immigrants like the Morris family entered Ellis Island for what was referred to at the time as a "six-second medical exam." A doctor looked over each passenger, and if he felt the passenger needed further investigation, he wrote a chalk letter on their clothes, the letter and placement representing different concerns:

X high up at the front side of right shoulder—mental defects

X farther down on the right shoulder—disease or deformity

X within a circle—some definite disease

B—back problems

G—struma (swelling in the neck)

H—heart problems

Pg—pregnancy

Ct—eye disease

After each Morris had a medical exam and assuming that all of them were deemed healthy, each one had an eye exam and a two-minute interview/interrogation that would have been conducted with an interpreter, as their language was Romanian. When the interview was completed to the official's satisfaction, each member of the family got his or her landing card and was sent to exchange their Romanian money—probably lei—for American currency, and then they would have bought their train tickets to St. Louis to finally see C. Morris at 1100 Twenty-Third Street.

I thought a lot about their entry to the United States. Whenever I travel to other countries and have to go through customs, I invariably get nervous. Even though I am traveling for vacation or work and never have live animals or some illegal kind of artisanal sheep's-milk cheese, I'm still worried that some official will pull me out of line and throw me in a foreign jail. Like maybe I went to a farm in my sleep and have a zucchini stashed in my luggage. I think about the bravery these people had when they left everything they knew for a new life in America, and I doubt very much I would have taken the risk, even if there was a C. Morris waiting for me at the other end.

Viki, Barbara, and I wondered who this mystery relative might have been, so we headed to the Missouri Historical Society Library's shelves that were filled with city directories, the telephone books of the nineteenth and early twentieth centuries. These directories listed every person with a telephone line in alphabetical order along with their addresses and sometimes even their occupation and workplace. The St. Louis books are called *Gould's St. Louis Directory*. We started with directories from 1902, 1903, and 1904 and went through them carefully—and came up with nothing. We went back through the previous eleven years, 1891–1901. There was no C. Morris. No Morris at 1100 Twenty-Third Street. The first time that Guerson Bernhart (now George Bernard) Morris appeared in the phone directory was 1918, where it simply listed his profession as photographer. No other Morrises appeared. In 1919, it listed George's profession as photographer at Grand-Leader, a St. Louis department store that later became Stix, Baer and Fuller. Such stores often had little photography studios where the sitter could choose to have a picture taken with a chosen background— sort of the Sears portraits of the day. (I collect these types of photos, specifically images in which people sit on a large paper moon.) This discovery was the first confirmation that Guerson Morris had indeed been a photographer. Perhaps he really was planning to become a filmmaker. As a former film student, I knew the first films in the United States had been made in the early 1890s, but I didn't imagine that the small village in Romania where the Morrises came from would have heard of that (because of course I know everything about early cinema and Romania).

When I did a bit of research, I realized that, unbelievably, I was wrong. Cinema in Romania began before 1900, and at the time the Morrises lived there, there were numerous public screenings of movies made there. Romanian photographers turned cameramen were enthusiastically creating films. The first ones were called "actualities," which were documentaries and were less than a minute long. But they could have been enough to inspire someone like Guerson Morris. The first film was shown in Romania in 1896, six years before the Morris family left for the United States.

So what we learned from the directories: In 1919, George B. Morris was a photographer at Grand-Leader. But his daughter Malvina, who was then twenty years old, also worked there as a stenographer, while Selma, twenty-six, worked as a saleslady at Hoover Suction Sweeper Company. They lived together in the same home. The family was putting down roots in St. Louis.

By 1920, George was photographing people at a private studio—no longer at Grand-Leader. Malvina was a bookkeeper at Grand-Leader, while Selma was listed as a saleslady at Frank Adam Electric Company. There were no listings for Marcella or Ruth. This was the same for 1921 (except now Selma was working at Bensinger Furniture and Stove Company as a saleslady). Marcella appeared in the directory in 1922 as a stenographer, while Sam, the lone Morris brother, was listed as a musician.

And that is the year the guides end. In 1922, all of them lived together at 4740 Newberry Terrace, St. Louis, Missouri. But it must not have been an overly joyous reunion, because it didn't quell the resentment the sisters had for Sam throughout their lives.

Once we were done at the historical society, Viki took us to the building where the Jewish Shelter Home orphanage had been when the Morris sisters were alive. It was located in the Shaw neighborhood, which was quiet and filled with trees and Victorian homes. The former orphanage was a grand and cheerful brick building with dormer windows and a large front door set back from a starched white porch with pillars and a flight of stone stairs. There was a brilliant late fall sunset that gave the windows a warm, golden glow. It was nothing like the dark Dickensian orphanages I had in my head: It looked like a large private home, doing its best to appear happy.

As Barbara and I headed back to our hotel, Viki told us to call

Jewish Shelter Home orphanage, St. Louis

if we needed anything, and I promised I'd be contacting her to help with my search. I kept that promise. I frequently emailed her questions I had about how to find information. When in 2017 I read about the vandalism and desecration of a Jewish cemetery in St. Louis (though not the one the Morrises were buried in), I sent her a note. She said it was a tragedy and they were very upset about it. She told me the then governor of Missouri (who was the state's first Jewish governor) was helping with the cleanup.

THAT NIGHT AT THE HOTEL, when I got into bed, my head was filled with the little Morris children. So much of their lives must have been informed by this early trauma, and it was doubled by the fact that they were too ashamed to tell anyone about their mother. The children must have thought they weren't going to be in the orphanage for long, and it would seem that one of Clara's three sisters—my great-grandmother Martha, in Manhattan, or her other sisters Rebecca, in Montreal, or Rachel, in New Jersey— would've taken them in.

I know that my grandmother had taken in her brother and other relatives when they needed a place to stay, even though she and my grandfather lived in a small apartment in New York City. My dad told me about different uncles who slept in his room when he was a boy and he would have to sleep on the couch. That's what families did in those days: They helped each other.

Why wouldn't my grandmother's mother have taken care of the

Marcella, Malvina, and Ruth Morris

Sam and Selma Morris

Selma Morris

Marcella Morris

Morris children? The story in my family was that the sisters were angry later in life about being left to fend for themselves without support from the rest of the family, and they were obviously angry with their father: The meager grave in the cheapest section of the cemetery was proof of that. Had their father ever tried to arrange for them to live with other family members, or was he just too ashamed to admit that he needed help supporting his family? Or maybe he really believed he was going to get them out of the orphanage soon and he didn't want to send them so far away. I hope that was the case. The alternative that he knowingly abandoned them is too horrifying to contemplate.

What was unavoidable was that the Morris sisters must have had to face the shattering feeling of being unwanted—first by their homeland and then by their father.

Yet there are clues that there was love as well. In a family album that my cousin Bobby has there are several lovely photographs of Sam and Selma and Marcella, and one of Marcella, Malvina, and Ruth, which Guerson took sometime before 1910. The pictures are so beautifully crafted that it's clear great care went into them. Nobody will ever know what Guerson Morris was thinking when he took them, but looking at these photographs today, more than a century later, I don't think there is a question that he loved his children.

ELEVEN

Clara Doesn't Live
Here Anymore

The next day Barbara and I met Larry Harmon, who gave us a tour of what had been the St. Louis County Lunatic Asylum (though the name was changed to the St. Louis Insane Asylum just before Clara arrived). The building wasn't far from the orphanage; had the children ever visited their mother, or did they even know she was there? The building was constructed in August 1864 by local architect William Rumbold. His idea was to create a structure that brought to mind imperial Rome, which is why it's topped with a dome, albeit a cast iron one. He had fine marble pillars imported from Italy for the front portico. The place definitely looked like what it was, beautiful but serious. Until recently it was the St. Louis Psychiatric Rehabilitation Center, but those offices moved to a newer building, and when we visited, it was mostly empty. We went inside and saw framed newspapers from the hospital's opening: a two-page spread from the *St. Louis Post-Dispatch* on January 3, 1904, when alienist (as psychiatrists were then called) Edward C. Runge, the asylum's superintendent, was "driven from the hospital" because he was "fettered by political influencers" to keep dishonest and incompetent employees and who "subjected him to repeated humiliations." Well!

We started our tour in the basement, where Larry told us "the most serious patients were kept." There were rings that hung from the walls, and I asked Larry if patients had been shackled. Larry said they had. There were showers at one end that the inmates were held under. Whatever the truth was about what happened here—whatever treatment or punishment the patients endured— it was a dank, dark, and somber space, and one I didn't want to linger in for too long. I did notice there were storage boxes stacked along the walls, and I kind of wanted to see if any of Clara's records were in them, but I didn't look. The only census record in which Clara was listed with her family in 1910 (it must have been early in the year) asked how many births she had and how many live children she had. The answer that was recorded was eight births and five living children. So she had three babies or small children die. It would have happened before she came to the United States sometime before or between Sam, Selma, and Malvina. Such loss would have been enough to throw me into deep despair I don't know that I'd ever recover from.

I let Larry and Barbara go ahead of me as we walked past dirty walls of white brick and saw the obscured keyhole-shaped windows that would have let in very little light, and I began talking to Clara in my head. I told her how sorry I was that she had been sick and that she had to leave her children to come to this place. I knew that she had been a good mother to her children and that she had endured so much pain and heartache over the course of her life, more than anyone should have to put up with.

As I moved along the corridor, with Larry and Barbara far ahead of me, I got a very strong feeling of someone saying, "I was so frightened."

At the turn of the twentieth century, psychiatry was at best a rudimentary arm of medicine. I'd researched the treatments for the mentally ill from that time, and they were, to say the least, limited. There was the ever popular "fresh air" treatment—basically being walked around outside (usually on the hospital's grounds)—as well as hydrotherapy, where patients were either thrown into a pool of cold water (it was supposed to shock them out of their insanity) or strapped into dunking devices or "bath boxes," where patients were immersed in water up to their necks. It was actually seen as an improvement over restraining patients in straitjackets. Women seemed to be particularly subjected to these kinds of treatments. By the 1930s, doctors often performed lobotomies, surgical operations where an incision is made into the prefrontal lobe of the brain and some of the brain is actually removed. (The way they were performed involved an instrument that looked like a small ice pick that went through the eye socket and into the brain.) The procedure was barbaric and ineffective and yet was performed into the 1970s.

Claire had told me that Clara was never able to leave the hospital, which makes me think she probably was lobotomized. Had anyone—her husband? Her children?—come to see her?

We toured the rest of the building and walked all the way up into the dome. During the tour Larry told us that in 1963, the city of St. Louis needed space to construct a four-story building, and officials chose a lot right in front of the Dome building, where it would block the view of the asylum from the street. People didn't like to see it, it seems. A friend of mine who grew up in St. Louis said that when he was a kid, the Dome building was the place his older brother used to taunt him with. If he didn't watch out, he'd be sent there. In 1968, two more floors were added to the front building. Can you imagine how it felt to have your entire hospital shrouded by a hideous cement-block monstrosity? The stigma of mental illness is a strong one. Larry showed me pictures of the building and told us it was demolished in 1998.

He asked us if we wanted to go into the dome. The patients wouldn't have been allowed to go up there, he said, but at the time it was one of the highest places to view the city. So we started the climb, first up some rickety stairs to some very unstable-feeling floors. We made our way up a wooden spiral staircase. As we climbed, I could see the colors of the sunset reflecting through the prism of windows in the dome and I recalled the story Ruth had written. Out the windows I saw her yellows and mauves and pinks and violets that "glowed for a space in pastel loveliness." At the top, with the city of St. Louis spread out before me, from the Mississippi River west toward the sunset, I looked for the angel with the "mother-look" as the colors faded.

As we climbed back down, I felt the motherless children and the childless mother, none of whom had been happy here.

ON THE FLIGHT back to New York, I rewrote the beginning of the Morris biography:

> Four Morris children, Selma, age nine, Sam, age seven, Malvina, age two, and Marcella, age one, came to St. Louis in 1902 from Romania with their mother, Clara, and father, Guerson. Two years later, in 1904, a sister, Ruth, was born, and six years later, on September 20, 1910, their mother was committed to an insane asylum. Two months later, on November 25, 1910, Marcella, age nine, and Ruth, age six, the two youngest Morris children, were put in the Jewish Shelter Home, an orphanage. Three months later, on February 23, 1911, they were joined by their sister Malvina, age ten or eleven. Four months later, June 29, 1911, Malvina was moved to the Cripples' Home for the summer. She returned to the orphanage and joined her sisters on September 6, 1911. May 30, 1912, a Dr. Horowitz writes a letter to the Morris

father, now known as George Morris, to get permission for Malvina to have surgery on her lame leg. October 31, 1912, she was admitted to the Jewish Hospital, where Dr. Horowitz and Dr. Hoffman operated on her. Four months later, on February 27, 1913, Malvina returned to the Jewish Shelter Home.

During those years, their sister Selma worked and lived with their father and their brother, Israel, known as Sam.

I'm not sure exactly when each child left the orphanage, but Ruth and Marcella both attended high school starting in 1917 and most likely were still in the orphanage, and left at some point before they graduated from high school in 1921. Malvina started working as a bookkeeper, and Selma continued as a salesgirl at several department stores and they were all working and living with their father in 1922.

Sometime in the years between 1923 and 1927, the Morris children left St. Louis. Sam moved to Texas, while Selma, Malvina, Marcella, and Ruth moved to New York City.

Those were the facts. The truth lay somewhere in them, I knew.

TWELVE

Reclaiming My Romanian Roots

When I returned to New York, I got a panicked phone call from Dr. Gyémánt. He was in Focșani, Romania, and couldn't find any records of my family. After talking further, we quickly realized that it was a translation error and that he was looking up the wrong name.

Later that day, he emailed me and said he had had better luck: The Morrises had in fact lived in Focșani and I could now plan my trip with confidence. I was relieved.

I have a long list of countries I've always wanted to visit. Romania wasn't on it, even though I had been a huge Nadia Comaneci fan in 1976 when she competed in the Summer Olympics, back when Romania was "behind the Iron Curtain." When the Soviet Union collapsed in 1989 and the Iron Curtain fell, the world changed, but my interest in Romania didn't. I hadn't seen many travel pieces on the glories of Bucharest, Romania's capital. But Romania was where the Morrises and my grandmother's family had come from, so that was where I headed. It would've been nice if I'd had Caribbean or Greek or French ancestors, but we don't get to pick our families or our ancestral homelands.

Because of commitments for the next several months, I didn't have a big window of time to go to Romania. It was pretty much December or never. The guide books warned travelers not to go then because the country is "dreary," "gray," "dark," and "bleak." But this was not a vacation, this was a business trip—a fact-finding mission.

I knew the two towns I needed to visit were Focşani and Râmnicu Sărat, both in Moldova, which has on and off been independent and part of Romania. In my research I learned that they were 185 kilometers and 148 kilometers respectively from Bucharest, but I couldn't figure out the best way to get to both places—car, train, or bus—and there weren't many hotels in either place. I emailed Dr. Gyémánt for suggestions.

He said in his opinion a visit to Focşani was worthwhile. "I recommend to visit the local Jewish Community. The name of the president is Mircea Rond, he is a journalist editor of a local Jewish newspaper. He can accompany you to visit the still existing Jewish sites like the synagogue and the cemetery. The address of the community is: Comunitatea evreilor, Oituz Str. 4, Focşani.

"As concerns Râmnicu Sărat, it is a town not far from Focşani and it is under the administration of the same Jewish community from Focşani."

Being the kind of traveler who panics if there's no turndown service, I was a little concerned that Focşani and Râmnicu Sărat weren't included in any of the *Condé Nast Traveler* or *Travel + Leisure* stories about Romania. There was a resort town on the Black Sea, just about an hour and a half away. Maybe I could just go there and, you know, take a ride to my ancestors' towns. If I found nothing, at least I would be in a nice hotel. Dan, my boyfriend at the time, listened thoughtfully to my plan and gently told me that what I was suggesting was dumb, really dumb. I knew it was, but I had tried to contact several different guide companies in Romania for help in getting me to and from Focşani and Râmnicu Sărat and no one was responding, so I was starting to feel as if I was traveling to another planet.

I mentioned the problem to a friend who studied for years in Prague and she connected me with a travel agent there who recommended a great guide in Bucharest, a young man named Valentin Gheorghe. I emailed him and he emailed me back quickly and soon an itinerary was born.

Dear Mrs. Klam,

I would like to suggest the following itinerary:

Day 1, Dec 5th
Arrival to Bucharest

Private transfer to your hotel (please provide me with the time of arrival and the hotel info). *I will provide you with a complimentary transfer, just to make sure you do not end up taken on a longer trip by a "too friendly" taxi driver.*

Day 2, Dec 6th

Explore Jewish Sites of Bucharest. *I believe it makes more sense to start here, where we have the largest Jewish community, with a Jewish History museum and 3 major synagogues. Having visited some sites here, we can cover the base of the story.*

Moreover, I also would not travel on Dec 6th because it is St. Nicholas Day and many will be running after presents or visiting relatives as it is the names-day of many Romanians.

Day 3, Dec 7th

Drive to Ramnicu Sarat (approx 2h15min)

Research in Ramnicu Sarat

On this day we can play it "by ear," depending on what you will find at each location. Focsani is only a 35min drive, so you can decide anytime for either-or.

Day 4, Dec 8th

Research in Focsani

Day 5, Dec 9th

Drive back to Bucharest. *Again, depending on what you will find at the sites in the country, having a car and driver, this day can be flexible. If by any reason a longer stay is necessary, we can even drive straight to the airport from Focsani.*

Day 6, Dec 10th

Transfer to the airport.

The above is what I believe makes the best of your time.

Please be so kind and give me your input. The above are only suggestions, open to changes according to your needs and priorities. Accepting or declining/changing the plan will not be met with a refusal to conduct the tour, but on the contrary, it be changed to fit your expectations.

This was my introduction to both the lovely Valentin and the affordability of Romania. I began to feel excitement about my trip; I would be walking where my ancestors walked.

I spent an inordinate amount of time selecting a hotel in Focşani. I found one with a website that had many pictures featuring a couple sitting at a table in the restaurant dining room, standing with a waiter showing them a bottle of wine, admiring the queen-size bed in the hotel room. They looked as if they answered a casting call for "guy who owns a suit and woman who has a dress" and they were the only ones to show up. Still, I liked the look of them and I made a reservation.

WHEN MY BOYFRIEND, Dan, and I booked our flights, we learned there were no nonstop flights between New York City and Bucharest, so we had to stop over in Warsaw, Poland, which somehow seemed to go with the tenor of the trip. For the couple of hours we spent at the Warsaw Chopin Airport—arriving early in the morning—there was no sign of sun, yet the place felt weirdly bright and dark at the same time, like the sun was in jail somewhere. And I was intensely aware of Poland's history: It was the location for several Nazi concentration camps. During World War II, Romanian Jews were brought to Chełmno, Belzec, Sobibor, Treblinka, Auschwitz-Birkenau, and Majdanek, all in Poland.

· · ·

THE HISTORY OF the Jewish people in Romania is not a joyful one. (The history of the Jewish people everywhere is not a joyful one, but I digress.)

There were only a small number of Jews in Romania until the nineteenth century, when many fled the horrors of the pogroms in czarist Russia and settled there. Unfortunately, Romania was not the refuge they hoped for. In Romania, anti-Semitism began to really escalate in 1821 with the first rumblings of Romanian independence from Russia and the Ottoman Empire. At the time, Jews were forbidden to settle in villages, lease land, and establish factories in towns. There were strict laws preventing them from wearing traditional dress, sending their children to school, and becoming Romanian citizens. In 1866, there was a major riot against the Jews in Bucharest, large numbers of Jews were robbed, beaten, and maimed, and the city's glorious Choral Temple was desecrated and destroyed. A law then was passed that said, "Religion is no obstacle to citizenship," but, "with regard to the Jews, a special law will have to be framed in order to regulate their admission to naturalization and also to civil rights" and "only such aliens as are of the Christian faith may obtain citizenship." This was followed by decades of anti-Semitism and the continuous systematic removal of Jewish rights. In 1877, Romania joined Russia to fight the Ottoman Empire of which it was part, and it successfully gained independence. With that victory came a new flurry of nationalism and worsening conditions for Jews. Up until then, Jews had been considered Romanian subjects within the Ottoman Empire, but now they were declared to be foreigners. Jews were forbidden to be lawyers, teachers, chemists, or stockbrokers. They were not allowed to be railway officials or work in state hospitals, and in 1893, Jewish students were expelled from state schools. Under the pressures of increasing persecution accompanied by political unrest and an internal economic crisis blamed on the Jews, a mass emigration began in 1900—about the time that the Morrises decided to emigrate to America. I've always wondered what that must have felt like. Was it a major topic of discussion? Were people all over town talking about whether to move or who was moving or who already had family there? Did it consume them or was it only a few people who kept their plans quiet?

I don't know, but here I was coming back (well, for a week) over a hundred years later.

THIRTEEN

Bucureşti, România

When we arrived at the Bucharest Henri Coandă airport, we spotted Valentin, a much younger man than I had envisioned. He drove us to our hotel in Bucharest, the Athenee Palace Hilton, which I had picked to offset the no-star Focşani hotel we'd be staying at in a couple of days. It was grand and beautiful, and Dan said it was exactly like the nicest hotel in Cincinnati and not at all European or Eastern European. But that was where he was wrong. Everyone who worked there was Romanian and you had to pay in Romanian lei, which I know for a fact they do not accept anywhere in Cincinnati. The hotel had a little bar that served English pub food, and the lobby, the staff, and everything in our room were five-star fancy, which I loved and Dan loathed. Also, the stuff in the minibar in the room was actually the price you'd pay in a candy store in 1979. Like a bag of M&M's was fifty cents and a giant bottle of water was seventy-five cents. My cousin David told me that once when he visited the Morris sisters in Southampton, Marcella gave him a large bag and directed him to their next door neighbor's farm to "pick"—I believe the technical term is "steal"—as many potatoes as he could carry. Given their interest in managing their food budget, I think they would approve of the minibar bargains.

We spent our first day in Bucharest with Valentin. When Dan and I traveled in Europe before, we liked creating our own schedules and keeping mostly to ourselves. We never used a guide. But I kept saying this trip was work, not a vacation. And after meeting Valentin, I wanted to bring him on all our future trips and maybe bring him home to live with us. He was informative and affable, and knew all the right people who could get us into all the right places. And he knew where to direct us for great meals and real Romanian atmosphere. The Morris sisters would have loved him, I was sure.

Bucharest in winter was cold and felt a little windswept. The Christmas decorations were out in full force, every lamppost decked in garland and bows and twinkling lights. A loudspeaker played what sounded like American Christmas carols in English, but none we'd ever heard before. One that was frequently repeated was "A Big Kid's Christmas."

It was snowy and dark even early in the day as we walked the city's streets. Though I completely bundled myself up into a long down duffle coat, wool hat, scarf, and gloves, the icy wind went right through me. So I was delighted for two reasons when we stopped at the majestic Romanian Athenaeum. First because it was warm, and second because it was also a breathtaking, neoclassical-style arts center.

Valentin spoke quietly to the people in the box office—they were clearly buddies. He told us that there was a concert rehearsal underway but that we could look into the theater as long as we didn't start singing or clapping along or otherwise making noise. So Dan and I peeked inside the door of the main concert hall and saw a full orchestra onstage in the midst of rehearsing a piece. The music was hauntingly beautiful and familiar. I wanted it to be the soundtrack of my trip, but my former steel trap of a mind couldn't place the name of the piece. I took a short video of it and when we got outside I texted it to my aunt Mattie, who is best friends with the conductor of the Cincinnati Ballet. Two minutes later she texted me back: "He said it's from *Scheherazade*." Of course, I should have known: I had played it on my flute for a seventh-grade band concert. The piece, he said, was "Kalendar Prince's Theme" and he even wrote out the notes we heard. After we left the Athenaeum, I hummed the melody as we walked until Dan told me to knock it off. Valentin was too polite to say anything, but I suspect he agreed with Dan.

WE WALKED ABOUT twenty minutes to the stunning, ornate Templul Coral, or the Choral Temple, the main Jewish temple in

Bucharest. Inside, Valentin spoke to a man who looked us over as he listened. They spoke in Romanian for a bit and then the man turned to us and spoke in perfect English. He was Gilbert Saim, the *gabai* of the temple, a sort of lay director who is not a rabbi. He asked us if we could Like the temple's Facebook page, which I did immediately. (I know the value of social media—it's like a twenty-first century version of tipping.)

Gilbert talked as we looked around. It wasn't really a tour because we could see everything from the spot we were standing. The architectural masterpiece was built between 1855 and 1858. The wealthier Jewish community in Bucharest at the time wanted a place to congregate and worship that was as magnificent as the synagogues in the major capitals of Europe. The Jewish community leaders chose as a model the Leopoldstädter Tempel in Vienna. Since the Leopoldstädter burned to the ground in 1938 on Kristallnacht, the Choral Temple is the only surviving replica.

Gilbert pointed to the balconies where the women would sit during services, this being an Orthodox temple. Above them was the hand-painted ceiling done in a Moorish Byzantine style in royal blues and pinks and gold. He said that when the temple was first built, there was always a choir that sang, which is how the Choral Temple got its name. In 1866 it was destroyed during the terrible pogrom, but a year later it was rebuilt. He explained that prior to World War I, wealthy Jews were the exception in Bucharest. Most synagogues were not like this one, Gilbert said, but instead looked like simple houses.

I was interested in what happened to the Jews in Romania after the Morrises left, because this could have been their fate if they had stayed. Gilbert said the current Jewish community in Romania is between 9,000 and 17,000 out of a population of more than 19.5 million. Before World War II, the number was 850,000. Some 450,000 Romanian Jews were killed during the Holocaust by Hungarian and Romanian fascists. After the war, many emigrated to Israel. Israel actually made a deal to pay a "ransom" to the Romanian Communist government for its citizens to emigrate there. The amount of ransom depended on each immigrant's level of education and social rank.

After a brisk five-minute walk we ended up at the Great Synagogue, also called the Polish Synagogue. It was built in 1845–46 by the Polish Ashkenazi community that lived in Bucharest. Ashkenazi Jews are from Eastern Europe as opposed to Sephardic Jews, who are from the areas around the Mediterranean Sea. The Polish Synagogue is no longer a functioning synagogue, and when we visited, it housed a large exhibition about the Holocaust. When we entered, we came across a group of old men with yarmulkes who were sitting around talking in the dim light. Valentin bowed and explained to them who we were. Then Valentin turned to us to say that all these men were Holocaust survivors.

A tall, thin man with a long, gray beard slowly stood up to take us around. I told Valentin to tell him that we could just look on our own, and he did, but the man shook his head and said he wanted to take care of these very special visitors from New York. And then he winked at me.

The man came over to us and stood with his hands clasped together and told us (through Valentin) that the exhibit was put together to show what life was like for Jews in Romania before, during, and after World War II. He told us that "Holocaust" means "burning completely" or "complete destruction."

The exhibit was a collection of carefully arranged photos, documents, and signs. The first pictures in the exhibition showed Ion Antonescu, Romania's authoritarian prime minister and ally to Hitler during the 1930s. He was "the worst man to us," our guide said. He shook his head angrily and Valentin translated, "Antonescu governed through extermination and destruction." The man pointed to a collage of Romanian newspaper clippings that reported the Antonescu government's discriminatory declarations. "He cut off the Jews from economic possibilities, leaving them with no financial freedom, but they had to pay *extra* in taxes!" the man said.

We saw photos of trains crowded with passengers. "One hundred fifty thousand Jews were deported from North Moldavia," the man told us. It was a chilling piece of history to learn: North Moldavia was where my family had come from, and we were headed there tomorrow.

The man continued walking past pictures, stopping to point out a photograph of people leaving the town they lived in on foot. "They couldn't take anything with them," he said.

I looked at Dan. I had always told him that my grandparents said the reason my grandmother had so much good jewelry was because Jews have had to leave places with just what they had on. You couldn't stash a Rembrandt in your pocket. At least with diamonds and gold, they'd have something to sell when they got to wherever they were going.

"They were forced on foot and they became exhausted and sick from the inhuman hygiene," the man told us. He stopped and looked at us. "These events were administered by Antonescu and the people who helped him."

He paused at a display of train schedules and pictures of people jamming into railway cars. The man pointed to a yellowed map. "Jews from the Northern Transylvania territory were given to Hungary through Hitler's Second Vienna Award in 1940. They were all deported by 1945 by the Hungarians and sent straight to the concentration camps in Auschwitz-Birkenau, where they were exterminated. In Northern Transylvania, there were one hundred sixty-six thousand Jews, and one hundred thirty thousand were killed."

The man looked at a photo of a beautiful young girl wearing the striped uniform of the camps. He spoke to Valentin and I heard him say, "Elie Wiesel."

I nodded and told them, "Yes, I have read *Night* many times."

Wiesel's first book was about his experience as one of the Transylvanian Romanians deported to Auschwitz.

The man nodded back at me and said something else.

In response I said, "I have no words for it."

Valentin translated and the man nodded again. We understood each other.

DAN AND I looked at the rest of the exhibit, and when we were done we thanked the men and said our goodbyes. As we were leaving, a wave of emotion washed over me. These gentlemen— these Holocaust survivors—were in their nineties. Soon time or illness would take them all. I felt both gratitude and sorrow for all of them, and in that moment I especially missed my grandfather, whose family had fled Bessarabia, which had been part of Moldavia, east of Romania. When he was alive I used to ask him questions about every aspect of life before I was born. What movies did he like? What did he do for fun before television? Did the Jews in the United States know what was happening to the Jews in Europe during World War II? He answered my questions so patiently, so kindly. Standing in a former synagogue and seeing the remnants of the horrors that had been inflicted on people his family may have known, I realized how painful my questions must have been. While it's so important to remember, it can be difficult, too.

. . .

I ASKED VALENTIN if we could head somewhere upbeat, and he pointed us toward Strada Cluceru Udricani. On the way we passed a large bust of Vlad the Impaler, the inspiration for Dracula. Valentin told us that he is actually something of a hero in Romania. I asked him why he has such an awful reputation. "Very bad publicist," he said.

We found ourselves at the door of Caru' Cu Bere, which translates to Beer Wagon. Its bright, festive jolt instantly made it one of my favorite places in Europe. Built in 1898, the neo-Gothic building has a vaulted ground floor richly decorated with brightly colored paint, stained glass, mosaics, and carved paneling. Music was playing, the waitstaff danced around the room in traditional Romanian costumes, and the taps were flowing with the Romanian beer Ursus. It was sort of a Romanian version of a German biergarten. This felt like a vacation.

The Morris sisters traveled quite a bit as adults. I had found their travel documents online, and they had been to Lisbon, Paris, Cairo, Cuba, the Netherlands, and London, but they never returned to Romania. This seemed like the kind of place they might have enjoyed.

We sat upstairs on a balcony overlooking a luminous, grand Christmas tree. A cherubic waitress presented us with tall, multi-paged menus, and Valentin used his to shield us from a neighboring table where he said a disgraced politician named Gabriel Oprea was sitting. He had been an interior minister who had recently resigned after protests against him. A policeman in Oprea's motorcade had been killed. After we ordered, Valentin giddily posted the sighting on his Facebook page.

After dinner, we walked back to our hotel and planned to meet with Valentin the next morning for the drive to Focşani and Râmnicu Sărat.

I had emailed and Valentin had called the synagogue in Focşani several times in the weeks leading up to my trip, and neither of us had gotten any response. We decided that we were going to just show up there and see what we could learn. (I realize how silly that sounds, but I didn't feel as if we had another choice.) We just hoped we would find something when we got there.

FOURTEEN

Focșani

The next morning on the two-hour drive to Focșani, Valen-tin told us about his work as a tour guide all over the world and his life growing up in Communist Romania.

"Prior to the revolution, my parents had some friends who were smuggling things through Yugoslavia, as Yugoslavia was just a bet-ter Communist country than us," he explained, chuckling. "They were able to get blue jeans, which was a big thing back in the day. So I was bragging about it in school and the principal found out about it and called my mom, and she was terrified, but it just turned out the principal wanted a pair, too!"

He also talked about his grandfather, who had been in jail for six months. "After 1947 when the Romanian king, King Michael, was coerced into abdicating, the change came. And by 1949, because of nationalization, everything was confiscated from people. Everything became state owned. My grandfather owned some horses as he was working the land for others. And the horses were taken away, and he received that message loud and clear, but then he was given a bonus of six months in jail to think about what he had done"—owning property.

We talked about the fact that Communists didn't recognize religion, but people still built churches and synagogues and set them far back from the road so as not to attract attention. There were a lot of steps people had to take to preserve some semblance of control in their lives.

As we drove down the highway, Valentin told us about seeing bands of Rroma people. "When I was a kid, they were still travelers, and would go from village to village selling various things, sometimes for money, sometimes for barter, for food. This was my first encounter with the Rroma. And when I was a kid my grandmother told me, if I didn't behave, she would let them take me with them! So they became scary to me. Like storybook witches. You would always see them at the borders of the village, basically camping out. You'd see them with these horse-pulled wagons. We were taught to have this animosity toward them. If you were misbehaving you were said to be behaving like them. We couldn't imagine they had the same values we did. But that was because they had difficulties integrating, let alone assimilating."

We talked about the similarities between what happened to the Jews and the Romani. He told us that Romanians are sort of seen as "lower status" in Europe, and when tourists from Western Europe meet him, they don't expect him to be smart and capable, which made me mad. Valentin struck me as personable and incredibly well informed about Romanian history and even the specific dates of events. He could do whatever he set his mind to, I was sure. He was more than a guide, he was a teacher, and I found myself writing down everything he said. I know that if he ever visited the United States and we took him around the country, I would say something like, "Yes, our Civil War occurred sometime between, oh, 1700 and 1940, don't quote me on those dates . . ."

We arrived in Focșani, a city of about one hundred thousand people northeast of Bucharest, in late morning and headed straight for the synagogue, which was located on narrow Oituz Street. The building was of a slightly dingy white stone, with tall windows and two Stars of David and a Torah carved into its facade. There were a couple of bare trees and a chain-link fence with stone pillars painted a dark cranberry color in front. There was a sign by the door that said "Federația Comunităților Evreiștie Din România Comunitatea Evreilor Focșani," which means "Federation of Jewish Communities of Romania Focșani Jewish Community." We went up to the door, which was also behind a gate, and knocked. There was no answer, so we knocked again. Still no one answered.

My come-what-may attitude was starting to alarm me. The three of us talked about whether we should find our hotel and then come back. As we were discussing it, a woman in a kerchief opened the door. Valentin spoke to her in Romanian and explained who I was and that I was hoping to meet Mircea Rond, who was the president of the Community of Focşani Jews. They had a further conversation and eventually Valentin turned back to us. He told me that Mr. Rond wasn't there, this was his wife. He would be available the next day. I asked if we could set up a time and she said 10:00 a.m. She went back inside and Dan, Valentin, and I looked at each other. Our plan had been to meet with Mr. Rond today and he would tell us what to do and where to go. Now that it would take place tomorrow, we still had a lot of time left today.

Valentin suggested that we go to the Office of Vital Records in Focşani to see if we could learn anything there about the Morrises. One of the details that I had observed about Romania, a country I was falling in love with, was that everywhere you looked in big cities and small towns there was a mix of glorious European architecture: beautiful stone buildings that made your heart soar and were a match for any in Paris, Vienna, and Prague; and buildings in various states of degradation—graffitied, crumbling edifices or abandoned completely (the Communists' intention was to destroy anything with historical value)—in which you could still see what they had *been*. Before the Communist era, Bucharest was called "the Little Paris." Now a big part of the city was blanketed by ugly, Soviet-era, Stalinist-Brutalist concrete-block monstrosities that looked like despair.

The synagogues I saw were the former, elegant and stunning. The vital records building was the latter. And not just in form, but in function as well.

We walked up a staircase to the office, and the line for assistance hit us midway up. The walls were painted institutional green; there were no adornments except signs in angry capital letters with a lot of exclamation points. I imagined they said YOU'RE DOING IT WRONG! GET OUT!

At the top of the stairs was a small glass window that an attendant opened a crack to speak through and then snapped closed immediately after. She had Crayola-red helmet hair, wore heavy, brash makeup, and had a pair of cat-eye glasses on a chain around her neck. She looked like a character from a Pixar film.

Valentin approached the window to see what he could find out. The woman looked aghast at such a breach in procedure and opened the window to yell at him. He spoke back and she closed the window and then vanished.

He looked at us with amusement. He, along with the person whose turn it was, stood at the window waiting for her return for nearly twenty minutes. When at last she came back, she addressed the other person and ignored Valentin. One of her colleagues, a man, appeared, and Valentin tried to ask his question to him. The man spoke without looking at Valentin (too much effort, I guess) and left.

Valentin then walked back to us and said that we would have to put our request in writing and wait for someone to contact us in eight to twelve weeks. Then we would be able to return to wait on the line with the other sad people.

I asked Valentin if this was what Communism was like. (America has such bullshit bureaucracy, too, but this had a more strident feel to it.)

"Yes, so we have no information about your family, but you now know what it felt like to live under Ceaușescu," Valentin said.

It was dark outside when we left, but we had the Morrises' address from the Romanian birth certificates, Centrala Street 36, and we decided to see if we could find the house.

There is no longer a Centrala Street in Focșani, but by locating a map of the area from the year 1900, we were able to track down where it was. We drove to that part of town, which was pretty desolate except for a group of small, abandoned houses that looked as if they were built in the mid-nineteenth century. When we pulled up to them, one of them had moonlight streaming down on it, and I decided that must have been the Morrises' house. It appeared long abandoned, and the lawn and shrubbery managed to look simultaneously dead and overgrown, like something out of *Sleeping Beauty*. Standing on the street where the Morrises lived as a young family full of hope, I couldn't help but feel that when they left this behind they felt some certainty that life in America would be worth all it took to leave here. Did they ever regret their decision?

I took some pictures and got back in the car, and Valentin drove us to our hotel.

Dan and I decided to have dinner at the Soho Pub, a Romanian interpretation of a typical English pub that was just across the street from our hotel.

We walked into a huge, modern, clubby-looking place. It was

pitch dark. A young woman came out of the kitchen and turned the light on. She seemed surprised to see us.

"Can we have dinner?" I asked in English.

She shrugged and clearly didn't speak English, so I used my five Romanian words and she pointed to all the tables (we had our pick). This type of experience rarely happened when we traveled in big cities—it was almost always possible to be understood. As strange as it was, I felt we were getting the sense of what it must have been like for people entering America unfamiliar with the language and customs: hostility disguised as indifference.

When the waitress came to our table, we ordered hamburgers. I pointed in my guidebook to the translation of "well-done meat"— "carne gătită bine făcută" because I wasn't really a meat eater, and if I were, I would prefer it didn't resemble anything meat-like. Dan indicated that his burger was not to be well done.

The waitress left and we went back to talking about our day. We talked and waited. And waited. And waited. After about an hour, the waitress reappeared and brought one burger to the table. We waited and then I called her back over and said, "Two burgers." She looked very disappointed in us. She had not understood that we each wanted our *own* burger, so she went back to the kitchen and we waited some more. Eventually another burger emerged from the kitchen. To my surprise, they were delicious—almost worth the ninety-minute wait. Or maybe we were just starving. After, we paid our check and left a large tip. The woman watched us go, locked the door behind us, and turned off the lights. I wouldn't have been surprised if we were the only customers for the whole week. We certainly were the only patrons that night.

The next morning on the way to see the synagogue, Valentin explained that people didn't go out to dinner much in these small towns because most of them couldn't afford to, and definitely not on a weeknight. Which would explain why our waitress was so surprised to see us.

We arrived at the Focşani synagogue and the door was opened by the jovial, robust Mircea Rond, with royal-blue eyes the same color as his sweater and a rim of white hair that circled his bald head. He walked us into the "office" of the synagogue, which was sparsely furnished with some old desks in two corners, and in the middle of the room was a kitchen table covered in a red-and-white-check plastic tablecloth. To one side of the room stood a prayer stand, which is usually placed in a synagogue to the right of the ark of scrolls. At one of the desks sat an older woman in a wool ski hat and scarf (it *was* cold in there), and she was looking at documents through a magnifying glass. She never acknowledged us. Mr. Rond's wife was there again, too.

Valentin asked Mr. Rond if he spoke English and he said, "Yes." To that his wife said quickly, "No, he doesn't." He shrugged and smiled, and everyone laughed. Mrs. Rond told Valentin in Romanian to translate or we would be here for a week.

We sat at the table and Valentin explained to Mr. Rond that I was looking for as much information about the Morris family as I could find. He nodded knowingly and I later found out that people coming in search of their roots was very common here.

Mr. Rond explained that when the Communists came to power after World War II, they took all the records and archives from all of the religious places, Jewish and Christian, so there was very little to show us. That was a disappointment: I'd hoped to get a sense of what life had been like here for a Jewish family like the Morrises.

There was a lot of talking between Valentin and Mr. Rond. We had now gone to several places with Valentin, and I realized how much I liked having to speak through an interpreter. So much of the time people say everything in a way-too-long, convoluted way,

Focşani synagogue

and the interpreter has to listen, and as he's doing that, you can smile and stare off into space and think about what you're going to have for dinner. Usually the interpreter comes back with a few words of explanation, and boom, you missed a big lecture but still get new information. It's the best of both worlds. But here I wished I understood Romanian.

Mr. Rond asked if we wanted to see the synagogue. When we told him that we did, he got up and went over to one side of the office, where he opened a set of French doors into a large room that was the sanctuary. He explained the synagogue had never been renovated, so it still looked much as it did when the Morrises came here.

The room was on the small side for a Jewish sanctuary, seating maybe sixty people or so, but the ceiling was very high and colored a pale blue that had gold hand-painted Stars of David on it. The walls were peach hued with more gold stars painted on them, and there were balconies across from each other. Just below the ceiling there were small circular windows on all sides, each with a Star of David on it, and in the front, an ornate ark of scrolls, pale blue and gold, and above it a large chandelier with bulb lights. Above it the eternal light hung. The sanctuary was even colder than the first room: I could actually see my breath, but I couldn't help feeling the warmth of the place.

The place was like a smaller version of the synagogues we saw in Bucharest, but untouched by time. I imagined Guerson Morris filing into the wooden pew for the last time, looking up at the stars, while Clara and the daughters looked down from the balconies (the women's section), each of them wondering what their new country would be like.

We returned to the kitchen table and Mr. Rond explained (with Valentin translating) that the Jewish community of Focșani dated back to at least the second half of the seventeenth century. A synagogue had been built on this spot in 1827 and was later destroyed by an earthquake. The one we were in—the one the Morrises would have known—was finished in 1896.

In 1899 there were 5,954 Jews in Focșani. Today there were fewer than 30. Mr. Rond ran the occasional service (though he's not a rabbi). He said that several years before we visited, a man whose family had come from the town brought his son back to be bar mitzvahed in the synagogue. He tried to find a video of the ceremony on his computer to show us, but he couldn't locate it, and I realized again how easy it was to lose sight of the past.

I asked what life was like in Focșani for Jews at the turn of the twentieth century and if he thought the Morrises left because of anti-Semitism. Mr. Rond said he didn't think that was likely. Though anti-Semitism existed, it wasn't what drove Jews from Focșani. They simply would have been looking for a better life, which fit with the story of Guerson wanting to be a movie director.

Mr. Rond went to a cabinet and took out some homemade local wine. Valentin told us that in December, when the wine is new, they call it must (pronounced moost). It's basically the first fermentation of the wine, a kind of Romanian Beaujolais nouveau, when it has all the sugar in it. Romanians are very proud of it because it's only around for about a week and then it's gone for the year. You didn't want to offend someone by not drinking their must.

He poured glasses for us. Valentin toasted us and proclaimed, "The show moost go on!" and I took a sip. While I like wine, even sweet wine, I thought my teeth would fall out from the must's sugariness. Dan managed to drink his—probably because he's from the Midwest and incredibly polite—so I shoved mine over to him while Mr. Rond went over to an old cabinet with a glass door. Dan courageously downed mine as well.

Mr. Rond brought back to the table several large and very old books that appeared to be some kind of ledger. He sat down again and told Valentin that when he arrived in Focșani, he didn't know much about the Jews who had lived here, but then he happened to find these ledgers and papers tucked behind a toilet in the bathroom. Someone must have hidden them there from the Communists.

"What are they?" I asked.

He looked at me and in English said, "Books old. People dead." Valentin shrugged and laughed.

Mr. Rond kept going. He told Valentin they contained all kinds of information about the Jews in Focșani. Addresses of families, births and deaths, the grades of the pupils who studied in the synagogue. And the synagogue had a copy of a book called *1789 Rules for Jewish Workers*.

He opened up one of the ledgers. Delicate, creased pages were filled with columns of boxes, and in each box were handwritten lists of names in ancient inky handwriting. Some boxes had one name, some had more. It was hard to decipher the faint tiny letters, but Dan, Valentin, and I each took a book and looked through them carefully, turning each page slowly, keeping our fingers away from the writing.

Mr. Rond said something and Valentin translated. "These are the forgotten people remembered."

Despite a thorough search, we didn't find any Moritz (which is Morris in Romanian), and Mr. Rond thought it was possible that when the Morrises lived in Focșani, their last name was Guerson. We did find a Moses Guerson who lived on the same street as the Morrises and who died in 1912, but we couldn't determine whether he was a relative. I showed Mr. Rond copies of the birth certificates the researcher had found for the Morris children, and in those the last name was Moritz. But he said what we would consider a last name would depend on who was writing a name in the ledger at the time. He pointed to the name of the witness who had recorded Sali Moritz's birth, and said something to Valentin and laughed. Valentin told us the witness was seventy-four years old. He may not have known what he was doing. (Seventy-four in 1900 was a lot older than seventy-four today.)

We asked Mr. Rond about the synagogue in Râmnicu Sărat. He gave us directions—the town was about forty miles away—and told us there was a man there who would open it for us and could also take us to the old cemetery in town.

As we got ready to leave I realized that Mr. Rond was my link to the Morrises, and to my grandmother, and to my Romanian past, and that this was probably the only time I would ever see him. The thought made me want to cry, which I did when he hugged me as he left and promised to email me the video he had tried to find. (Spoiler alert: He didn't and he never responded to any further emails from me. However he *is* now my Facebook friend and likes pretty much everything I post.)

Râmnicu Sărat was the town that Selma and Sam were born in; the Morrises must have moved there when Clara was pregnant with Malvina. Râmnicu Sărat was the next town of any size south of Focşani, so the move wouldn't have been too much.

Synagogue in Râmnicu Sărat

We met a gentleman who had been tipped off by Mr. Rond. He unlocked the door for us.

The synagogue in Râmnicu Sărat was very much like the one in Focşani. It had been built in 1855 and had never been renovated. The entry room was filled with Holocaust documents and old books stacked on tables and windowsills.

The walls and ceiling of the sanctuary also were hand painted in pale blues and corals with gold Stars of David. There also were tiny murals and gold eagles on the walls, and the chairs were upholstered in aubergine velvet. At one time it must have been stunning, but now there were water stains and large cracks in the walls. It looked as if everyone left this place one day and forgot to come back.

Valentin pointed to a side table. On it was a red velvet cloth that spelled out in gold thread "MORITZ SEIFLER." Mr. Rond had told us that as with English, Morris was both a first name and a last name.

I HAD COME to Romania to find out about what life was like when the Morris family lived there in the nineteenth century and what may have caused them to leave. Life in the first half of the twentieth century must have been extremely terrible to have caused the Jews in Râmnicu Sărat—indeed, across Europe—to leave so quickly. Or was it the belief that life was just so much better in America?

What would the Morris sisters' lives have been like if they'd stayed in Romania? Would they have survived World War II?

Would Clara still have gotten sick? Would Guerson have abandoned his family? Would Malvina have gotten any help for her leg?

Standing in that forgotten synagogue in an overlooked town in a little-visited part of Romania, I realized that so much of life is made up of how we deal with the choices we've made and the choices others have made for us. As we go through life, we make decisions on what we should do and how we should live. Should I go to school? Get married? Whom should I marry? What job should I do? Where should we live? After a certain point, you realize that you must contend with those choices, as they frame the future you'll have.

We left the synagogue and headed to the local Jewish cemetery. I told Valentin that the Morrises had taken a steamship from Southampton, England, to New York, and wondered if he knew how they might have gotten there.

He answered quickly: "On foot!" Sometimes Jews leaving Romania had a horse and wagon, but many of them walked for part of the way. They believed they were coming to America, a place of fortune, freedom, and a future, so they did what they had to in order to get there. And when they arrived at the boat, they traveled in steerage, which was all that most of them could afford and which was an additional nightmare. Ship companies made money from numbers, so people were crammed in the lower deck of ships, where lights were kept on all the time, hygiene and privacy were nonexistent, and the passengers couldn't see the sky. The conditions were terrible, but Valentin told us that the people who left

Romania were not the worst off. The Romanians who emigrated were far from rich, but if they were truly poor, they were left behind. It was those who had enough money to have hope who emigrated.

We arrived at the spot that the Jewish cemetery was located, which was not far from the synagogue in Râmnicu Sărat. There was a huge building in front of it, apparently some kind of factory, and we were told we had to walk through it to get to the cemetery. This felt wrong: It wasn't how cemeteries were placed or organized anywhere else I've been.

We went into the factory, which seemed empty: Nobody was around. Suddenly an older man in blue coveralls emerged from a hallway. Valentin told him that we were looking for a cemetery, and the guy nodded. He took us out a side door and pointed to a chain-link fence just ahead.

The cemetery gate was kept closed by a stick with a wire around it. Not exactly high tech. We lifted the wire and the entire gate collapsed, falling into several pieces at our feet. We stepped over the pieces and put the gate back together like we were rebuilding a house of cards.

Cemetery in Focşani

Inside the cemetery, the stones were a mess, shattered and uprooted. Portions of the place were so overgrown with brambles that I had to use a stick to get near enough to the stones to read them. I had never seen anything like it. The entire place looked as if it had never been maintained, though I knew it had also been a casualty of many earthquakes.

I walked over to one side of the cemetery to gather stones for the graves and gasped. In the grass were animal skeletons. Dozens of them. Mostly dogs, I assumed. It was a disturbing find to stumble across.

I picked up stones to put on whatever graves were standing. I was looking for the Morrises, but I wanted to give anyone I could find a stone. When I did find an intact gravestone, the letters on it were so faint and worn that almost all of them were impossible to read.

The sadness in this place was overwhelming: The people buried here had been forgotten by the living. I hoped their souls were off somewhere having a nice party. The dogs, too.

It was around three o'clock and by then we'd spent a couple of hours there and none of us had found any Morris or Moritz graves. Our plan had been to stay in Focşani another night, but really we had seen and done everything we could. Valentin offered to drive us to Transylvania, but we decided to head back to Bucharest. I was kind of desperate to get back to the bustle of a city and the cheer of a joyous beer wagon.

We said our goodbyes to Valentin and I told him to please come to New York and bring his family. He said he would love to. We chatted a bit about travel and I mentioned we were thinking of going to Prague and Vienna the following year, and he said to let him know, that he was there a lot (which we did and actually met him for dinner in Prague, but that's a story for another book).

That night in Bucharest Dan and I went to a traditional restaurant called Vatra.

When I walked in, there was something about the smell and the decor that reminded me of my grandma Billie's house: There were scents of cinnamon, coriander, dill, and rosemary; the air was warm; and the light was golden and cozy. A red velvety wallpaper covered the walls, and traditionally dressed musicians walked around and played guitar and lute and some kind of pan flute. We had delicious eggplant spread and hot bread, and fried cheese appetizers and warm vegetable soups, and then I had my favorite chicken schnitzel and Dan had stuffed cabbage. Like any minute now Grandma Billie would appear wiping her hands on her flowered apron.

As Dan slept that night, I lay awake thinking of how I was here with this man I loved who very possibly would become my second husband and that there are so many different ways to go through life. I chose to have someone along for the ride, while the Morrises blazed through life on their own, content with each other. There was a time in my late twenties when I had lived alone so long that I thought I might not meet someone and get married, and imagined my life on my own. It very easily could've gone that way.

Maybe if I had lived with my sisters I would have felt less of a longing to meet someone.

THE NEXT DAY the only place I really wanted to see was the Museum of the Romanian Peasant. (This wasn't officially a business visit, but I wanted to try to get a sense of how most Romanians lived during the time that the Morrises lived there.) It was a long walk from the hotel to the museum, but we enjoyed it, as it gave us the opportunity to see more of Bucharest's grand architecture. But when we got to the museum, we found it was closed for renovation. The gift shop, however, was open. It sold blouses and skirts and handmade beaded jewelry and scarves and hats, little dolls and refrigerator magnets. I wanted to buy everything I saw. I had a feeling I wouldn't return to Romania, and I wanted to take home something of it with me. After spending way too long deciding, I picked out a couple of gifts, but nothing that really satisfied me. Maybe that was impossible.

That night we ended up back at Caru' Cu Bere for a last beer. As I sat there, while I knew I was ready to go back to my life, I felt a longing for a place that no longer existed.

FIFTEEN

Cousins and Commodities

Romania was so important in seeing where the Morris sisters—and I—came from: our shared history, and how what happened to them at the beginning of the twentieth century informed all of our lives in America. There is so much that we can't be sure about in our family history, even if we have the facts. But now I had a glimpse of the life that Guerson, Clara, and their children left behind and what they might have been looking for in America. I felt my grandmother Billie there as well, and I had a sense of what they must have brought with them: their meager belongings, of course, but also parts of themselves that were intangible—family recipes, traditions, memories, faith.

While the search in Romania was more complicated and less definitive than I'd hoped, I imagined that further research in the

United States would be different. Maybe, I thought, I'd walk into the New York Public Library and find the Morris sisters there, fully formed from all the detailed information about them that I could call up from the library database. (Cue the gods laughing at me.)

When I returned to New York, I emailed a historian at the New York Public Library's Division of United States History, Local History and Genealogy and explained what I was looking for—any information on the Morris sisters and their lives—and where I was in the dark, which was pretty much everything about Marcella's career. A few days later a research librarian responded with a few pages from Ancestry that I already had and suggested that I look through the financial company's annual reports. (The what?) And if Marcella had spoken at the White House, I could check the Congressional Serial Set (1817–1980). (Again, the what?)

I wrote back to say thank you but left out that I had no idea what he was talking about. I told him I would be visiting the library soon and discovered I didn't need an appointment.

Regarding my understanding of all things financial, I believe the technical term for me is "dum-dum." My father was a financial planner, and my husband (reader, I married my boyfriend) writes about financial situations for big banking companies, so you would think that some of their expertise might have rubbed off on me. Yet nothing has. It might be because I have never had any of my own money so I have not needed to figure out what nifty ways I can invest or what types of IRAs I should open. In terms of the stock market, bonds, and commodities, every bit of it is not just unfamiliar to me, it is deeply upsetting. It's in another language that I feel I should know and realize that I probably never will. While money makes the world go round, it's also kind of boring to me. I want to throw rocks through the business section of every newspaper I come across, being the financial Neanderthal that I am. This is not a trait I am proud of, believe me. At the same time, I know that I've reached an age where I am more comfortable with words than I am with numbers, and I'm okay with that deficiency.

I now realized that I wasn't going to be able to research an important part of the Morris sisters' story if I didn't understand the world they, particularly Marcella, lived in.

I was still not sure where Marcella worked as a trader. In her later life she was self-employed, and in all of the censuses that I researched, her profession was listed as bookkeeper, and in the 1940 census she was listed as a secretary in an advertising agency. (The censuses beyond 1940 were unavailable.) The New York Public Library had sent me links to many archives but said there was a lot more in the library that wasn't digitized, so it might be worthwhile to come in person.

I really wanted to know more of Marcella's work story from my family. My father's cousin Bobby, who is Claire's brother, was the executor of the Morris sisters' estate, and I am very close to his two daughters, Sherie and Carole. Bobby lived in New Jersey and Florida like Claire did. When I was first thinking about this book in 2007, I emailed Bobby (who was then seventy-nine years old) and asked him for any information he had about the Morris sisters. This was the email I got back:

Hi, nice hearing from you.

Four Morris sisters and their brother set out from Montreal in the cold of winter sometime at the turn of the 20th century to California. Their mother had tuberculosis and father, an unemployed photographer, had reasoned that the weather there would be good for mother and the newly formed movie industry would provide opportunities for employment. Upon reaching St Louis, the mother got sick and died and the father put his five children in a Jewish orphanage, telling the children, he will get a job, pick them up and resume their trip to California. In short he never returned, Marcella got out of the orphanage, went to Cleveland and got a filing job with an investment banking firm. The firm recognized that she had a great memory of trading symbols and trained her as a commodity trader. Her expertise was in pork bellies. In fact at the beginning of World War II, she was summoned to Washington DC to testify on winter corn and pork bellies since at that time it was a staple of the average diet. She thrived in the industry, endured enormous animosity from a male dominated field, and made lots of money. All of her sisters lived together for their entire lives, mostly doing business with females. Never recovering from their father's betrayal. Leaving the bulk of their money for the benefit of female related causes. Hope this answers your inquiry. Love, Bob

Reading this, I realized that it must have been Bobby who had written the sisters' biography for the Southampton library—he was the Morris Foundation! Though he had gotten the information from them, I knew that parts of it weren't accurate, but I now knew what questions I wanted to ask. So I called Sherie to see if I could arrange a meeting with Bobby in Maplewood, New Jersey, where he and his wife, Eileen, have a condo. (They live primarily in Florida but come to New Jersey to see their children, grandchildren, and great-grandchildren.)

Sherie told me that her father had been having some significant memory loss, so I shouldn't expect too much. I made a date for the following Monday and started work on my list of questions.

SIXTEEN

The Berkowitzes of Maplewood

During the drive from New York to Maplewood, I thought about my family and how nice it was to be close to my second cousins, and I wondered how much Bobby would remember. Which led me to think about my own memory. When I was young, I had a ridiculously retentive memory: I could remember details about people's lives, meals I had eaten, the dialogue from entire movies. It was almost like a party trick. Then in my forties, around the time my first husband and I were divorcing, I lost it (my memory, not my sanity). I can still remember details that normal people recall, but my memory is no longer one of my superpowers. If in thirty years my niece decided to write a book about my cousins and she started asking me questions, what would I be able to tell her? Even now, so many details about my past are completely gone. My mother, however, remembers everything everyone ever did, especially if it was not good. She puts it in her mental "book." I am fairly certain she could get full-blown amnesia and still remember the kids who came over at noon and how their mother didn't pick them up until 11:00 p.m.

My expectations were in check—I didn't know what I'd find. I was really just looking forward to seeing them. It had been about five years.

I walked into the condo and Eileen said, "My God, you got so tall!" I had just turned fifty. It was one of my favorite moments.

Carole and Sherie laughed, and I told them I did think I had a little growth spurt recently.

Eileen had had a genealogist do a family tree for her several years ago, and she gave me a copy of what had been found. Eileen also showed me a photo of a beautiful painting of flowers that she had in Florida. Malvina had painted it, she said.

Bobby was now almost ninety and he looked well and was so happy to have us all around him. But as we talked, it was obvious he wasn't sure about many details, and I realized that I already had most of what I was going to get from his memory.

It was a bit past lunchtime so we went right out to a local diner and caught up on more-recent events. We talked about Sherie's new granddaughter and Carole's kids and who everyone had spoken to. It was so much fun talking with relatives you loved and actually enjoyed spending time with, a benefit of researching family. I thought of the Morris sisters and imagined they probably just sat around sometimes enjoying each other's company.

Seated, from left: Billie and Willie Klam and Malvina, Ruth, and Selma Morris at a Berkowitz bar mitzvah in 1966

On my way back to New York, I decided I needed an expert who knew the financial world to explain it to me. I had the ideal candidate: my father's cousin Herbie. He and my dad actually lived together during various times of their childhoods growing up in New York City during the Depression, and he has always been more like my uncle. I've adored him ever since I was a kid.

Herbie served in Germany during the Korean War from 1953 to 1955. He came home and with the GI bill was able to get his college degree and then an MBA, both from NYU. After teaching business at St. John's University, he became a successful stockbroker, financial researcher, manager, adviser, and partner in the company that became Citicorp, and he owned his own financial services firm. If anybody could explain the intricacies of the financial world to me, it was Herbie.

We set up a time to talk. I wanted to hear his thoughts on Marcella Morris, the financial sister—and anything he could remember about any of them.

Like my father's other cousins, Herbie has a home in the Northeast (his is in Westchester County, north of New York City) and a home in Florida in the same community that Bobby and Eileen live in.

"Hiya, dollface!" he said when he recognized my voice on the phone. Everyone should have someone in their life who calls them dollface unironically. (He also signs his emails "Unky Hoib," which might be the best signature ever.)

We chatted about family for a bit. He told me he had just gone to Staten Island to the United Hebrew Cemetery, where his parents and my great-grandmother and some other relatives are buried. He told me I should go out there, too. I asked if the Morris sisters were buried there.

He laughed. "Nooooo, they were cremated and . . . disposed of. They didn't want anyone pissing on their graves."

I asked what he knew about Marcella.

"I knew all four of the sisters," Herb told me. "Your grandparents, Billie and Willie, held a seder every year for Passover in their house in New Rochelle, and Malvina, Selma, and Marcella would come. Malvina was very badly crippled, as you know; she could walk but it was terribly difficult. I can recall vividly the moment the seder was over, Marcella would head for the stairs and go up to the second floor to do her work, I guess trading commodities."

My grandparents had moved to their house on Fern Street in New Rochelle when my dad's sister Susie was born. My father was entering his senior year of high school and when they moved, they pulled him out of his private school in Riverdale, New York, that he commuted to from their Harlem apartment. The house, I remember, was dark, with paintings on the walls of old Jews and the old country. Later, when they moved to Florida after they retired, everything in their apartment was white or Lucite, including the matzoh container (the Lucite box had "Matzoh" printed on it). They had gone from dark to light.

Listening to Herbie, I imagined Marcella setting up a workspace after dinner in the upstairs bedroom with the fuzzy olive-green flowered wallpaper and using my grandparents' black rotary phone that sat on a doily on the night table.

"Julie," Herbie admitted, "she wasn't pleasant." It was clear he was no fan of Marcella's, and I was interested to find out why.

I told him that Claire had said Marcella was the secretary of J. P. Morgan and they had had an affair, she furnished his New York City apartment, and they talked about what stocks to buy. I had already determined that it could not have been J. P. Morgan, because he died in the St. Regis Hotel in Rome when Marcella was twelve and still in the orphanage in St. Louis. I wanted to know if he had any better intel.

"This is the story as I know it," Herb began. "Somewhere along the line Marcella became a secretary to Harold Bache. Harold Bache was the nephew of the founder Jules Bache, who succeeded him at Bache and Company, which you probably know as Prudential-Bache. Let me tell you, at that time Bache was huge, second or third largest in the entire stock market in terms of dealing with retail clients. So purportedly she was Harold Bache's secretary. What the hell did that mean? I don't know, and I'm not being cute."

So the stories about Marcella having an affair and talking stock tips with J. P. Morgan were probably about Harold Bache—and even then they may not have been true. I kept thinking about what work must have been like for her. Everyone said she was surly; maybe she had to be that way to fight for her place as a broker in the male-dominated world of Wall Street. I can't imagine how many men told her to smile more. I have no doubt that much of her unlikability came from the fact that she was a woman who behaved the way she wanted to. I always think that of the four Morris sisters, Marcella would have been the least likely to be my friend. (I try to be liked and don't like people to be mad at me.)

"I don't know how the hell they got to New York and how she got in with Bache," Herbie said. "Suffice to say she was very, very,

very successful. And there were no women on Wall Street then. Just very, very few."

Herbie attempted to explain the commodities market to me so that I had a rudimentary sense of what Marcella's job was. (There was a moment as he explained it when I understood it, but don't ask me to repeat it here.)

I asked Herbie if he thought that Marcella had a trading account when she was a secretary. This was my theory about why she had several lowly jobs when she was supposed to be making a lot of money. Everyone said she was a genius. Herbie agreed.

"I was then coming out of . . ." He paused and called out to his wife, Sandra, "Hey, hon, when did I start with Marcella? Undergraduate or graduate school? Graduate school? Okay." He returned to his story: "Someone hooked me up with Marcella. You know, I knew them from the seders. Malvina and my dad were very close. And we adored Malvina, she was the normal one. She was as lovely a human being as you could get your hands on. So I guess Malvina connected me with Marcella, or maybe I had the audacity to call her for help. I just needed a job. So Marcella introduced me to a guy who served as her broker at that point. Julie, I can't remember what I had for breakfast yesterday, but I remember his name: George Breen. I don't know what firm he was with. But he was her broker and he handled all her business, and the last thing that SOB wanted was for me to become a broker—he didn't want to share her business. Having said that, he certainly did talk to me and gave me time because she must have put the screws to him. So he got me an interview at Maryland Casualty Insurance Company in Towson, Maryland. Sandra and I had a long discussion. Neil [his oldest son] was either in the crib or about to be in the crib. I didn't want to go to Maryland, Sandra had a job here, she was a teacher, and that enabled us to eat! I had just finished my master's and I didn't want to go. I didn't take the job, which pissed Marcella off. And she didn't talk to me again other than nodding to me at your grandparents' house."

Herbie continued: "So here we are. Now let's jump to around 1980. What year was Marcella born?"

I told him 1901.

"So she was close to eighty herself. I got a call from her after not hearing from her for over twenty years, okay? (Hey, San, how old did I say Marcella was when she called me that time? Eighty or ninety?) So at that time, thirty-five years ago, being eighty was improbable. It wasn't like today. She knew I had done very well, I was a partner. My secretary comes into my office and says, 'A Miss Morris is on the phone.' And I said, 'Who?' She says, 'Miss Morris.' I'm thinking, 'What the hell?' And then I say, 'All right. I'll take the call.' So I pick up and she says, 'Herb?' and I say, 'Yes, Marcella.' So I don't know the exact figure, but she asked for credit for either a million or twenty million or fifty million to trade commodities. She wanted to open an account! To trade! I'm not joking!

"I said, 'Marcella, I have nothing to do with commodities.' She said, 'Herb, I've followed your career and I know if you wanted to make this happen, you could make it happen.' Well, (a) I didn't really give a flying *hmm* for her; if it was Malvina and she needed ten thousand dollars, I would have found it and given it to her. But this one, I wouldn't give her the perspiration off my butt." Herb sounded like Jackie Gleason.

"She said, 'Herb, take care of it, I know you can.'"

"I said, 'Marcella, I'll get back to you in a day or two.' I waited a day. I didn't call anybody, I didn't twist one arm. I called her back and said, 'I'm awfully sorry, Marcella, I can't help you.' So she starts rattling off a number of the firms she traded with. And I said, 'I did the best I could, but I cannot accommodate you, but thank you for calling, it was nice to hear your voice, and be well.' And that was the last time I talked to her, ever. And then when everyone started the drumbeat—you know, when she was on the way out—everyone wanted to get a piece of this action. Believe me, if I could have stomached her, I would've taken a shot [at getting into her will]. But I was on the outs with her from the day that I refused to go down to Maryland."

I asked him what he thought about the fact that Marcella was so successful and one of the few women who'd had a flourishing career on Wall Street, why he thought I couldn't find anything about her.

"Julie, I never, ever, ever saw her name in print," Herb said. "When I mentioned her to people at the time, no one ever heard of her. I read all the financial literature—magazines and whatnot— and I never saw her name. I knew people, I knew a lot of top people, and I never heard about her from anyone except the people in our family. I think maybe it was just that she was not liked. That's my guess." I feel angry on her behalf thinking of how many unlikable men get profiled ad nauseam.

I asked him if he remembered hearing about other women on Wall Street. He gave some thought to the question before replying.

"I'm sure there were some, but not many. There were just no women on Wall Street, and for her to rise up like that was truly a phenomenon. In the annals of finance, you just didn't see women."

I told him I was going to go to Prudential-Bache and ask the company if it had any historical records that mention Marcella.

"I wouldn't bet on it, nobody gives a shit," he said. "Honestly, Julie, our industry was not known for keeping adequate records for anything."

While I knew he was right, I hoped he'd be wrong.

SEVENTEEN

The Harvard of Jews

J ust about everyone I interviewed about the Morris sisters eventually brought up Brandeis University. Claire, Bobby, my dad, and Herb all had said the Morris sisters gave millions of dollars to the Jewish university in Waltham, Massachusetts.

Herbie said that he thought the sisters' donations might have started in the 1960s. He said they were well known to abhor men and he thought they didn't want their money to go to male students. He thought that their money was only to benefit women and women's studies. The feeling among the family was that the Morris sisters had hated their father for putting them in the orphanage in the first place and never taking them out again, but since they all went to live with him when they aged out of the orphanage, I thought their donations to Brandeis women might have been for some other reason. Or maybe that wasn't the case at all.

Herbie said he heard that Marcella was giving money to Brandeis and insisting it went to women's studies and women students, and that Brandeis objected, so she and her sisters stopped contributing. But he wasn't sure whom he heard that from, and I knew now that many of the sources for such stories were difficult to pin down and their accuracy was questionable. I hoped that any interaction the sister had had with a university would be well documented and that maybe I could speak to someone at Brandeis who'd dealt with Marcella and her sisters over the years.

I emailed Brandeis Donor Relations and explained that I was looking for any information regarding the donations of my relatives for a book I was writing. Someone in the department responded that she did in fact have information on the Morris sisters, but she would have to find out through the legal department what she was allowed to release to me. In the meantime, she wondered if I had contacted the Morris Foundation. Yes, I said. The Morris Foundation was my cousin Bobby.

About a week later I got an email from her:

Hi Julie,

Sorry it took me so long to get back to you. There were a few people I needed to check with on this, but I've finally got it all straightened out. Here's what I can do for you.

First, I am allowed to share with you that Marcella Morris and her sisters and brother made bequests to Brandeis that totalled a number in the high six figures. There was no specific designation, and so it was used for the University's Annual Fund, or to relieve any immediate needs the University had during their lifetimes. A few of them made small gifts, but the total was less than $20,000, over a number of years, to various programs, and in small amounts.

However, I understand now where the millions figure you had came from. It is possible that at one time your relatives may have had estates with a combined worth of that much at one point in time. We were never given paperwork to confirm this amount, or confirm that it was coming to Brandeis. Over the years, as your aunts aged, their estate may have been drained to support their living and healthcare expenses. So what may have once been an estate of that size may have dissolved for a number of reasons. This is only my guess from the paperwork I have reviewed (and which you will see) and from our experience with other donors in similar situations. Your relatives' only connection to Brandeis University was through our first president, Abe Sachar.

Apparently, they grew up with him in St. Louis and maintained the connection. The bulk of the paperwork we have deals with the will of Ruth Morris. I don't think it's of interest to you at all (no biographical information at all)—and it conveys a lot of direct information about the gifts she and your family made to the University, which as a rule we cannot share the details of. However, we also have a few notes over the years that were written to them, as well as by development officers that convey some biographical information. I can give you copies of these. (Again, from time to time there is sensitive information in these that I will need to black out, as we generally don't give them out and they are not intended for it—you are the exception to the rule.) However, I should be able to provide you with a few copies of documents that provide some biographical information about your relatives. I'll make copies and black out what I need to and send to you soon.

So despite the family's stories that we took as truth, the Morris sisters didn't actually give millions of dollars of Marcella's money to Brandeis. But the high six figures was certainly something, and even more since the contributions were made at least forty years ago. (I would like for someone to give me some high six figures today.) Apparently the sisters also didn't specify that the money needed to go to educating women. Everyone in the family claimed that the sisters hated men and that they were strong and independent—and how important this narrative was to their myth. I already knew that their father didn't drop them in the orphanage and leave town for Los Angeles and that they lived with him when they got out. He never left St. Louis. When the four Morris sisters first arrived in New York, they stayed with my great-grandmother Martha, their aunt, who was their mother Clara's sister. How much had she known about her sister, and her nieces going into an orphanage? Had she learned the truth of what really happened when they came to New York? She might have blamed their father or maybe she felt guilty for not taking them in. If she was anything like my grandma, her daughter, she wouldn't be shy about a strong and steady pummeling of her brother-in-law's character.

I'm sure the notion of Guerson Morris aspiring to be a movie director would've struck everyone in the family as ridiculous. Martha may well have talked to the rest of her family about what had happened and turned everyone against Guerson. The fact that the three oldest daughters lived only with each other and never married would have perpetuated this belief. It was neat and melodramatic, and explained what the people in the family couldn't understand.

A week later, I got PDFs from Brandeis University of what I was allowed to see. This is what it said:

Dr. Sachar

January 17, 1992

MARCELLA AND MALVINA MORRIS

Malvina (born 3-11-1900) and Marcella (born 9-17-01) Morris are the two surviving members of a family of five unmarried siblings. Their brother died in 1963; their sister Ruth died in 1978; and their sister Selma died in (?) 1990. They live in Southampton, Long Island, and virtually never leave home. Marcella recently stated that the family grew up with Abe Sachar in St. Louis.

Brandeis received small gifts [REDACTED] from the Morris Sisters in the 1950s. [REDACTED]

[SEVERAL PARAGRAPHS REDACTED]

Brandeis counsel met with the Morris sisters in New York in 1964 hoping to confirm their estate plans or establish a life trust. [REDACTED]

Following Ruth Morris's death in 1978, the university was informed that she too had left her entire estate in trust for the benefit of her sisters for their lifetimes, with Brandeis as the ultimate beneficiary, as their brother Samuel had done. Accountant Anthony Ullman indicated that

Brandeis was the ultimate beneficiary of all of their estates. [REDACTED]

Brandeis had correspondence but no personal contact with the Morris sisters during the 1980s: University officers met several times with accountant Anthony Ullman.

In 1990, Anthony Ullman informed us that he was no longer the accountant for the Morris sisters, as they had decided to let a relative (nephew or cousin), who is an accountant, handle their financial affairs.

[SEVERAL PARAGRAPHS REDACTED]

Both sisters have been hospitalized recently but the caretaker who answers the phone indicates that there are no serious problems and that a visit would be possible. Malvina, who spoke to me on the phone in December 1991, was perfectly [REDACTED] and cordial and asked that we try next month. She remembered the correspondence from President Thier, including the long letter explaining his vision for the University. [TWO MORE PARAGRAPHS REDACTED]

<u>CONTACT REPORT</u>

Date of Contact: June 5, 1992

Date Submitted: June 6, 1992

Department: Development/Planned Giving

Name of Prospect: Malvina and Marcella Morris

Affiliation: Friends

Address: Gin Lane, Southampton, NY 11968

On Friday, June 5, 1992, Vice President Dan Mansoor
and I visited Malvina and Marcella Morris at their Southampton home for several hours. Also present were Gloria
Smith and her daughter, Lauren, who have been employed as housekeepers and caregivers for the elderly
Morris Sisters for four years. Gloria Smith had spoken
with me numerous times over the phone during the moments in which I reestablished contact with the Morrises.
The Morris Sisters had obviously been looking forward
to our visit, were very happy to see us, enjoyed talking
about their family and old times over lunch and were
sorry when we had to leave. Their caregivers told us that
the Morris Sisters do have plenty of visitors.

As soon as we entered the house, Malvina Morris, who
is confined to a wheelchair due to lifelong hip problems,
introduced her sister, Marcella, saying "she is the brains
of the family." Indeed it was Marcella who had repre-
sented the family in all correspondence with their accountant, their attorney, and with Brandeis, in our files
and who was said to handle the family finances. [RE-
DACTED] She repeatedly explained that Malvina knows
more people than I do, "because I always had to work."
Marcella worked in bookkeeping and accounting positions
since the age of 16, while Malvina was kept from working
from time to time by her medical condition. Separately,
each person in the household told us that Marcella had

been the financial expert and Malvina was the more social person.

The Morris family is from St. Louis and they said that all family that they ever had are dead now. They said that they came to New York for the sake of better jobs. For at least 40 years, three of the sisters, Selma, Marcella and Malvina, lived together in New York and Southampton, staying permanently in Southampton sometime in the 1970s. Selma died there in 1991. (May 18, 1991, according to Gloria Smith.)

Both Malvina and Marcella talked a great deal about Brandeis University throughout our visit. They explained that Marcella herself had been unable to finish college (Washington University in St. Louis), lacking one credit toward the degree because she had to work. They knew of a "brilliant Jewish boy in St. Louis" who "could not go to college." They apparently lived across the street from Abe Sachar's father's business, and referred to Abe Sachar often, usually with an appellation like "that brilliant man," but clearly meaning Abe Sachar (for example, knowing that he had four sons and one of his sons had died).

[REDACTED] Marcella repeatedly stated that their brother, Samuel, who died very suddenly (at the airport on his way to visit them in Southampton in 1963) [RE-DACTED]. They are concerned about the cost of their constant healthcare.

Both sisters spent considerable time with us reminiscing about their brother, Sam, and the great legacy he had left to the university. They specifically spoke about the youth of the school and how it did not have the advantages of "the other school in Boston that's as old as the United States."

When asked later, the Smiths confirmed that the Morris Sisters have "talked about Brandeis all the time, since we've known them," talking about how it was "the first Jewish school" and "the first one to let everyone in."

I read over the documents several times. They felt similar to the minutes from the orphanage, detailed and written at the time the event occurred, not hazily recollected or disparate memories like jigsaw pieces from an unknown puzzle. The two points that jumped out at me were the way the Morris sisters got involved with Brandeis through Abe Sachar—a childhood neighbor—and that Abram Sachar was the first president of Brandeis. He took the job in 1948 after Albert Einstein turned it down. Sachar had been born in New York City in 1899 and was the child of Lithuanian Jewish immigrants. When he was seven, he moved to St. Louis, Missouri, where his grandfather was the chief rabbi of that city. It was there that Samuel Sachar, Abe's father, owned a clothing business on the same street where the Morris sisters grew up. According to notes from the Brandeis development office, Marcella and Malvina said Abe

Sachar hadn't been able to go to college, but he actually went to Washington University in St. Louis, and then Harvard, where he graduated Phi Beta Kappa, and finally Cambridge University, where he received his doctorate in history for a thesis on the Victorian House of Lords. So he certainly went to college.

Marcella graduated from high school in St. Louis in 1922, two years after women won the right to vote and were getting out in the world in greater numbers than earlier generations had. At the turn of the century, only 19 percent of college students were women, but by 1928 it was up to 39 percent. Still not a huge number and definitely not everyone could go. My father's mother, Billie, who was around the same age as Marcella, grew up in New York City and wasn't poor but did not go to college. My mother's mother, Pearl, who also grew up in New York City and was not only well off but also her parents' little princess, did go to college. She told me that her mother gave her ten dollars and she took the train to Columbia University and enrolled. On the way home, she ran into her friend Norma, who said, "Why did you sign up at Columbia? Everyone knows all the cute boys are at New York University!" My grandma Pearl went home and cried to her mother about this bombshell news, and her mother wiped her tears, gave her another ten dollars, and told her to go down to New York University and enroll there. (Which she did and she met a very cute boy there, my grandpa Saul.)

I knew that Marcella was working right out of high school, but

I wondered if she might have gone to college at the same time. Given her intelligence, it was possible that she might have gotten a scholarship.

I called Washington University and explained that I had a relative, Marcella Morris, who it seemed had been a student there sometime between 1922 and 1929, and wondered if there was some way to find her, even if she hadn't graduated. The very nice woman I spoke to said they actually had phone books for all the students and she could search them for me. A day later she let me know that she had gone through all the phone listings for those years and there was no Marcella Morris, but she told me that the Washington University yearbooks (*The Hatchet*) were now digitized and I could access them. I thought it would be around 1923 or so, but I decided to go further back, to 1917, and work my way through to cover all the bases. The yearbooks were not searchable; you literally had to go through them page by page and read everything. But they had every student enrolled that year—freshmen, sophomores, juniors, and seniors—with their names and pictures as well as all of the schools (nursing, law, etc.). I looked through each page of *The Hatchet* from 1917 to 1929, and Marcella was nowhere to be found. I studied every club photo and class picture, and she was definitely not there. I imagined that as smart as she was, Marcella must have found it extremely painful not to have gone to college. Did she see herself as the female Abe Sachar who might have had similar success in academia if she'd had the same opportunities he'd had? They were both poor Jewish kids who

Samuel Morris

grew up in Ward 23 in St. Louis. Abe was two years older than Marcella, so they might even have run in the same circles.

The other detail that struck me was the mention of Sam Morris, the sisters' only brother. Almost no one in the family mentioned him, and certainly none of the biographical information gave more than a line that he existed. They were always referred to in my family as the Morris sisters. What about the Morris brother?

Through my Morris sisters research, I learned that he was the oldest living child, born Israel Moritz in Râmnicu Sărat, Romania, on July 12, 1897. He emigrated with his family in 1902, and would have been fourteen when his mother was committed to the asylum in St. Louis, so he did not go into the orphanage. He received a draft card from the newly founded US Selective Service System in 1917, just at the end of World War I, when he was twenty-one years old, but did not serve in the military. In 1920, he was working both as a musician and an insurance broker in St. Louis. (So Claire was right that there was a musician in the family, but it was Sam, not Guerson.) When the Morris sisters moved to New York, Sam moved to San Antonio, Texas, where he met Esther Mary Pomerantz, the daughter of Polish immigrants. She went by Mary, and on July 28, 1927, her parents announced her engagement to Sam in the Houston *Jewish Herald Voice*. Mary was twenty-five and Sam was thirty-one. They were married on August 12, 1927, in Seguin, in Guadalupe County, Texas. In 1930, they lived in a small house in Seguin, where Sam owned a dry goods store and Mary sometimes worked as a saleslady. They had no children. On June 24, 1934, Mary was committed to the San Antonio State Hospital, which was formerly known as the Southwestern Insane Asylum. On February 17, 1935, at 4:35 p.m., Esther Mary Pomerantz Morris died at age thirty-two. The cause of death was listed as "Exhaustion Due to Insanity." She is buried in the Congregation Agudas Achim Cemetery in San Antonio, Texas. Her headstone reads "ESTHER MARY, BELOVED DAUGHTER OF LOUIS AND IDA POMERANTZ, JUNE 17, 1902–FEBRUARY 17, 1935." And in Hebrew it says "REST IN PEACE AND LET HER SOUL BE BOUND UP IN THE BOND OF ETERNAL LIFE."

There is no mention of being a wife, or the last name Morris, or her husband Sam.

I shed my share of tears during the researching of the Morris sisters' lives, but the story of Sam caught me totally by surprise. To have both your wife and your mother suffer from mental illness and be committed to asylums where they died was a horrific, unbearably sad coincidence.

In Judaism, the headstone isn't laid on a person's grave for a year because it's believed the soul is judged during the eleven months after death. The headstone is a sign of completion. So for a full year—and beyond—Sam was grieving alone, and maybe even being blamed or blaming himself for Mary's death.

For the rest of his life he remained a widower and lived alone in San Antonio. When he filed for naturalization in January of 1956, Sam wrote Mary's name on the form as his deceased wife, twenty-one years after her death. He worked as a men's clothing salesman, rented his home, and must have saved every penny he made, as when he died he left most of his estate to Brandeis University. Though he never amassed a fortune to rival his sister Marcella's, Sam used what he had to make life better for Jewish students at Brandeis, which he had chosen for its connection to Abram Sachar, and inspired his wealthy sister to do the same.

In 1963, Sam planned to visit his sisters in New York for the first time ever. He died at the San Antonio airport before he boarded his flight.

EIGHTEEN

FDR and NYC

I had been thinking about hiring an assistant to help me research the Morris family for two reasons. The first was that I saw how useful it was in St. Louis to have another set of eyes looking for details and following leads, and the second was that I was about to publish my fifth book, and my brain can't exist in two books at the same time. (I know there are writers who can do that easily; good for them.) I figured I would need someone who could look through documents, but I also wanted someone willing for us to do the research together, kind of like a genealogical Starsky and Hutch.

Alison was a graduate student and had been the thesis advisee of my friend Meg. Meg had been using her as a research assistant, too, and said that she was qualified and delightful and, just as important, had some spare time.

I contacted Alison and explained what I was doing, what I knew, and what I wasn't sure I could find without her help. Alison was fascinated by the project and had some good research ideas. We decided to meet at the New York Public Library in the genealogy room and together we'd dig around in the city guides and see what we could find of the Morrises' daily lives.

The Manhattan telephone directories for the years the Morris sisters were in New York (from 1930 on) were on microfilm. Reader, do you know what microfilm is? If you're young and grew up never being without a cell phone, the internet, or social media, you may not have ever used microfilm or even heard of it. Back when I was in school and we used our feet to propel our school bus and Dad ran a dinosaur in the quarry, we used microfilm in our liberry. The microfilm reader looks like an old black-and-white TV. (Or if that's not a visual you're familiar with, an old desktop computer. And if that's not a visual you're familiar with, then just stop it right now!) At a library you would request a certain reference book, and the librarian would hand you a box and inside was a roll of film. But it's not moving images, it's microimages ("micro" was a word used to describe high-tech devices back in the twentieth century). You thread the film into the machine, not unlike how I used to load film into 35 mm cameras in college (which I didn't do if I could help it even though I was a film major and it was a mandatory skill to learn).

Everything I needed from the New York Public Library about the Manhattan phone directory was in those little boxes. Alison heroically fixed the machine every five minutes when it did something weird that I'm sure I had *nothing* to do with, and she took responsibility when we were talking too loud and another patron shushed us.

We went through as many phone books as we could together, and Alison stayed to finish the job when I had to leave. What twenty man-hours of work got us were addresses. They were only for Malvina—Marcella and Selma lived with her, so they were not listed. And there were about twenty million Ruth Morrises. Even I wasn't foolish enough to search through them.

In 1930–31, Malvina was listed as living at 240 Waverly Place in Greenwich Village. In 1931–33, she was listed at 130 West 116th Street, which is near Columbia University. I wondered if it was actually Sixteenth Street, because they'd always lived in Greenwich Village, not near Columbia. By 1934, she was back downtown at 29 Charles Street, where she remained for the next thirty-two years, until 1966. The Charles Street home was a West Village six-story apartment building on what was and still is an incredibly charming block. Their apartment was a third-floor walk-up and, as I'd later discover, Ruth's was a brick town house nearby. This was when I first learned that all four of them didn't always live together, as the family story went. In fact, Ruth didn't live with them after the initial year.

When I went to see the buildings for the first time, it dawned on me that the Morris sisters were in New York City for the 1929 stock market crash and throughout the Great Depression. In the 1930s, the Village was an artsy, bohemian haven. Cafés and pubs filled with musicians, actors, and artists lined the leafy cobblestone streets. When I was in high school in the 1980s, my friends and I loved to take the train into Manhattan, and we'd head to the Village to visit vintage record and punk rock stores. Many of those stores are still there. I deeply admired the Morris sisters' choice of neighborhood.

In 1966, Marcella and Malvina moved to a brand-new, full-amenity high-rise at 360 West Twenty-Second Street in Chelsea, the neighborhood north of Greenwich Village. Alison and I were confident it was them because the phone number was the same as that at the Charles Street address.

The next day Alison and I went back to the library, and I read through books on women in finance while Alison courageously went through dozens of financial reports for J. P. Morgan, Bache, and Dean Witter, and *The Association of Stock Exchange Firms Annual Directory and Guide, The National Federation of Financial Analysts' Societies*, and *New York Society of Security Analysts, Inc.*, all with the goal of finding any reference to Marcella Morris.

There were no mentions of Marcella Morris in any of them.

I started to realize that it was entirely possible that I would not find anything anywhere about Marcella, though Alison and I agreed that it was highly unlikely the story of her visit to the White House was completely fabricated, and after looking at every possible White House document online, we decided our next stop was the Franklin Delano Roosevelt Presidential Library, in Hyde Park, New York.

THE LIBRARY WAS a couple of hours' drive north of Manhattan, and as we drove up there on a perfect late summer day, Alison and I talked about the fact that, growing up, she had lived on two of the same blocks as the Morris sisters, and we decided she had been destined to be part of this project.

We got to Hyde Park and went directly to the presidential library. No appointment was needed, but there were scheduled times that you could order materials. Because it's an archive of important original documents and artifacts all relating to the presidency of Franklin Delano Roosevelt, we had to follow a strict procedure. Our bags with everything in them had to be stored in a locker, though we were allowed to hold on to our cell phones. We were given pencils and pink sheets of legal paper to take notes on, which was all that we were able to bring into the library.

We told the librarian that we were looking for information on Marcella Morris, who had visited President Roosevelt in the White House, and we understood that she had spoken to FDR about winter corn and pork bellies, which were needed to feed the armed forces. (Pork bellies are exactly what they sound like, a cut of pork from the belly of the pig.) The librarian explained there were several files on agricultural meetings, and there was even a notebook where a White House guard had documented every person who came to see the president during his administration. We were allowed to get our first request of files immediately, but after that we had to order them at specific times. The library staff members would bring you a cart with the files, and you were instructed to use only one file at a time.

When the files arrived, the librarian showed us how to open and turn the pages so that we wouldn't damage these original documents. Inside the file folders, which were a very hard cardboard, were original copies of typed notes that were taken during every moment of Roosevelt's official business during his presidency. Alison and I sat at individual tables with one file at a time. It was extraordinary to look at not only the care and detail that had been put into the notes, but also the integrity of Roosevelt. His responses to whoever wrote to him were thoughtful and caring. One entry was "Thursday, February 12, 1942 Mr. Littlejohn—Farm Sec, Mr. Brunger—Re letter of use for his son, Miss Rebecca Rose-C.E.C.C. (home phone # 1199)." And "Wednesday September 10, 1941— Myrtle Sherrie told her her problems." And on and on. Some had physical descriptions (short man with glasses).

Going through the ledger page by page was a slow, tedious process, and it wasn't long before I was convinced we weren't going to find any information about Marcella. Still, it was impossible not to be impressed by reading documents that outlined Roosevelt's solutions to problems. In one file United States agricultural officials told him that there was a national shortage of eggs, and his reply was to reduce the price of chicken feed. In another letter he admonished someone for saying publicly that the war would end early because he needed factory production to keep running at a high level. And the same person also mentioned "a lot of loose talk about meat famine and a meat shortage for the coming winter." He responded to letters about victory gardens, and on September 11, 1944, he wrote to send food to the concentration camps in Poland.

The food production plan for 1944 said, "Our food plans for the future are, of course, predicated on the assumption that we must not only continue our shipments overseas but actually increase them. The war is by no means won, and the global effort must be continued and accelerated. The requirements for our armed forces will be increased, not only will they have a larger number of men and women than in 1943, but because more of them will be stationed in distant parts of the world. The average soldier or sailor eats approximately five and one quarter pounds of food per day—almost half as much again as the average civilian who eats only three and three quarters pounds per day."

I read executive orders, lists of food production, and letters from farmers pleading for help, which Roosevelt gave them. But I came across nothing about Marcella. Nor did Alison. After several hours of research, we admitted defeat and headed back to New York City. We decided that we could always return if we needed to.

On the drive back to New York, Alison and I talked through what we found and together we realized we weren't likely to find this piece of information at the FDR library. The conclusion was discouraging—I thought this lead had been so promising. Could it have been Harry Truman, not Franklin Delano Roosevelt, whom Marcella had met with? But as Truman's library was in Independence, Missouri, I decided to let it go. One research trip to Missouri per book was all I could handle.

The more I thought about the absence of Marcella from just about every public detail of her life, the more the feeling grew that it had been intentional on her part. Like the phone number being listed under Malvina's name. I also worried that my not being a trained genealogist or historian or even an experienced researcher was the reason I couldn't seem to find anything. The more I thought about it, the more I realized that even if she had been mentioned in some obscure financial document tucked away in a company archive or presidential library, she still wasn't mentioned in any newspaper article during her entire life or in any place that a layperson would have found her. And that in itself seemed significant.

Several days later, I saw that an event was being held at the New-York Historical Society library—an introduction to the library's genealogical resources by its librarian and then a presentation from the New York Genealogical and Biographical Society. This, I thought, could be a way for me to learn how to become an expert researcher—or at least a better one.

I signed up, and when the day came I showed up at the New-York Historical Society headquarters, on Seventy-Seventh Street and

Central Park West. When I arrived, I realized I was the youngest attendee by about forty years. I felt a spring in my middle-aged step.

One of the other attendees, a tall, gray-haired man in a tie, sweater vest, and sports jacket, told me that he was writing a family history for his children and grandchildren and that his family's lineage went back to New York in the 1600s. He looked pleased and confident about what he knew of his ancestors and his family's past. I told him he was lucky his task was so easy; mine was a challenge. Much more complex!

The presentation began, and the two dozen or so other attendees and I spent a couple of fascinating hours looking at the collection of materials that the New-York Historical Society had. There were maps from the 1700s showing almost nothing north of Fourteenth Street and a book that chronicled the street names in New York and what they had been changed to over 350 years. There was a logbook from the 1700s that recorded all of the African American babies that had been born, each mother's name, and chillingly, each mother's "owner's" name. There was also a large collection of letters from the New York Foundling Hospital, an orphanage created in 1869 by the Sisters of Charity for Catholic Orphans. Mothers had left these letters to explain the circumstances that had led them to the desperate act of leaving their babies. They were heartbreaking; some mothers knew their babies were dying and that they couldn't afford to bury them. (One letter said, "Don't be afraid of the sores on her face, it's only ringworm.") Others said that they had tried to find work but no one would hire them with the baby. Many said they hoped to come back for their children when life got better. Just the way the Morrises' father had likely hoped.

I realized that if the Morris sisters had lived in New York in the 1750s or the 1850s, I'd have much better luck with the resources of the New-York Historical Society. They just had so much research material that reached further back than more recent history, and in terms of genealogy, it's better if you are dead for longer, because more material is made public.

After the presentation, I introduced myself to the genealogist who'd given the talk and told her that I was looking for information about women who had died in 1978 and the 1990s. She knew exactly what I was talking about: with the rule that someone has to be dead for seventy-two years for the census records to be made public or for fifty years for vital records such as death transcripts to be available per the Freedom of Information Act, and there was no way around it unless I was the parent, child, or sibling of the person I was searching for. The genealogist questioned me about my research, and I explained what I'd done and was both happy and dispirited to hear that she agreed I had uncovered all the tracks that I could. There were no secret doors that I hadn't unlocked.

Then she said something that I really liked: "With genealogy, you rarely get proof, but you often get evidence." I had a lot of evidence.

She also said how important it was to look at the backs of photos. You never know what you'll find written on them, and that I should also write details (names, dates, locations) on the backs of my own photos for future generations. It reminded me of a picture my parents had of my grandmother as a young flapper in the 1920s, sitting on a fire escape in New York City. On the back she or someone else had written, "40 E 40th St. 1922," and it was captioned "The Human Fly." It also reminded me of the boxes of photos I have collected over the last thirty years that have nothing written on the backs of them. Except for my immediate family, I have no idea who many of the other people in the pictures are. I vowed to get help from people I know to identify and mark the photos up. There is nothing more confusing than finding a batch of photos of people and one rando in them you don't know and can't tie to the group.

At the end of the workshop, the genealogist handed us a list of websites—all of which I'd already visited—but she said sometimes it pays to look again. She also mentioned that when you get five thousand hits (possible answers) on whatever genealogy site, it's *the site's* algorithm that gives you the top hits it has chosen, so it is worth spending time looking at what the site may not have picked up on.

Equipped with this information and with more hope than when I'd arrived, I went home and started looking again at some of the sites I'd visited before. I put in Marcella's name. All the dates and places auto-filled, and the usual documents—census, travel manifests, etc.—appeared and this time I clicked on "Social Security Application and Claim Index." As I read it over, there was a small checkbox, which I had never noticed before, to request a copy of the original application. I clicked on it and was taken to the Social Security Administration website. The top of the page said "Electronic Freedom of Information Act Request for Deceased Individual's Social Security Record." I hadn't known I could do this, and I ordered records for Marcella and then for Selma, Malvina, and Ruth, filling in their names, dates of births, places of birth, parents' names, and of course each's Social Security number. Each record was twenty-five dollars for a photocopy or twenty-two dollars for a "computer extract." I chose the photocopy. It seemed like a steal.

While I waited the two to three weeks for the records to come, I returned to my research of women in finance in the first half of the twentieth century. Years ago I had read a great biography of Victoria Woodhull, who with her sister, Tennessee Claflin, were the first female stockbrokers on Wall Street, in the 1870s. Victoria Woodhull was also a radical female suffragette, a newspaper editor, and the first woman to run for president. The sisters were also very involved in the spiritualist movement. In the 1860s, Tennessee became the spiritual adviser to Cornelius Vanderbilt, the famed railroad tycoon, and rumors abounded that they were lovers. In 1870, Vanderbilt backed the opening of Woodhull, Claflin and Company Brokerage House. All the papers wrote about the scandalousness of petticoats among the bulls and bears. *The New York Times* headline was "Wall Street Aroused"—I'm not making this up— while *Harper's Weekly* called them "bewitching brokers." People clamored to get a glimpse of these women traders. (I love the idea of someone thinking, "What should I do today? I know, I'll go look at women stockbrokers!") It was said that Cornelius Vanderbilt gave the women stock tips that earned them the equivalent of $13 million in today's dollars. It should also be said that Woodhull and Claflin tapped into an underrepresented group of investors—wealthy women. Widows, society ladies, and even prostitutes all came to them not in spite of but *because* they were women. Late in the nineteenth century, a small number of financial institutions in the United States opened "women's departments" for women to do their business—manned by men, of course.

To no one's surprise, the walls of Wall Street were not moved by Woodhull's success: In the 1920s, there were still very few women on Wall Street and they were almost all in menial clerical jobs. Sylvia Porter, the renowned financial journalist, wrote an advice column in the *New York Post* beginning in 1934, but her gender was disguised behind the byline S. F. Porter until 1942, when the paper's editors decided her gender wasn't a hindrance and might actually be an asset.

During World War II, many women were recruited to fill the jobs of men in the armed forces in manufacturing, medicine, and education, but Wall Street still didn't believe women were up to buying, selling, and trading stocks, futures, and whatever else was for sale in the US financial markets. Post–World War II, there were only small numbers of women on Wall Street and they were still doing mostly clerical work. By the 1950s and '60s, a few women were able to break into some research positions. In 1967, Muriel "Mickie" Siebert became the first woman to purchase a seat on the New York Stock Exchange. It wasn't easy to do even then. She had to have two sponsors in order to buy her seat, and nine men she approached turned her down before she was able to find the required two.

Almost every book and article I read about women in finance mentioned how many of the women who were able to break into the trading side deemed it prudent to keep a very low profile, not overproducing or getting a lot of attention or ruffling any feathers. This to me seemed the most likely explanation for the absence of Marcella's name from the histories of the women on Wall Street. My family thought so, too: If Marcella was doing as well as she appeared to be, there was no benefit for her to call attention to herself. I kept saying that, but I still really wanted to find more.

The last place on my list to visit was the Rogers Memorial Library in Southampton, New York. I knew the Morris sisters had donated to the library because there was a Morris Meeting Room. I hadn't been in contact with the library since I'd gotten the initial (mostly incorrect) biographical material. But after all of the research I'd done, I figured that there might be some information that someone there could provide about how the library came to get the sisters' donation.

My friend Lauren is a librarian in Long Island, and she recommended that I email Beth Gates, a librarian at Rogers Memorial. (The person I had previously contacted was no longer there.)

About the Morris sisters, she said in an email, "Our meeting room is indeed called the Morris Meeting Room, and our Reference area is also named the Morris Information and Reference Center (see attached image of the plaque). I would be happy to dig around and let you know what I can find, and if you let me know when you are visiting I will gather materials for you."

She also asked me for the Morris sisters' address in Southampton, to see if there was any estate information. A few days later, Beth emailed me to say the sisters must have lived frugally because they weren't listed in any estate guides and that none of their obituaries appeared in *The Southampton Press*, the town newspaper. "Strange, if they lived here for 30+ years that they wouldn't have an obit in the local paper."

I told her that I had come across this issue again and again. The Morris sisters seemed to be very good at flying under the radar, alive and dead.

Beth said she found the files from their donation and I was free to look through them whenever I could get out there. She also suggested that a good place to find information on past residents was the Southampton History Museum, and that I should speak to Mary Cummings.

I called my aunt Mattie, who has a car and a house in Montauk, not far from Southampton, and asked if she wanted to go with me (that is, drive me out there, take me to dinner, and let me sleep at her house). She said she would be delighted, so we planned to travel the following week. In the meantime, I emailed Mary Cummings at the

Southampton History Museum and asked her if she had any records of the Morris sisters. She looked through the museum's collections and archives and found nothing. (Surprise!) She suggested that I contact the town historian, Zach Studenroth. I had a pleasant back-and-forth with him, and he asked me if my "ladies were with the Morris Studio, a local photo shop in business since the 1890s?" Unfortunately, my ladies weren't. He had a few other Morrises who weren't them, and then suggested I contact Mary Cummings at the Southampton History Museum. (And scene!) I had come full circle.

Mattie and I left New York in the morning and arrived in Southampton around noon. Mattie dropped me at the Rogers Memorial Library and went to look at patio furniture.

A smiling young woman with light brown hair and glasses, Beth Gates, greeted me and showed me the Morris Meeting Room. It was a large conference room with a long table, with "Morris Meeting Room" displayed on one wall in very large gold letters. I wondered if the library would let me rewrite the biography on the wall.

Beth took me to the reference room where there were a table and chairs, and brought me the files she had found. The first item I came across was a letter from April 10, 1995 (Malvina died in January of 1994, so it would have been just Marcella who was still alive), from the Morrises' lawyer (now long gone) that said, "I have a client that is interested in making a substantial contribution to your library. Please have a representative of the library contact me and arrange for a conference. Your prompt response is imperative."

It seemed that at the time the library was being rebuilt, the Morrises wanted to donate to help defray some of the costs. In the file were a few pages of handwritten notes from Marcella's lawyer requesting that the new conference room be named "The Morris Meeting Room" and the new reference area would be "The Morris Information and Reference Center." Another memo discussed the Morris sisters' financial distribution to the library, which turned out to be three trusts, each in the amount of $100,000. There were faxes back and forth between lawyers from the library and the bank and the Morrises, and on one of the faxes, someone had written, "Renaming the conference room??? This seems like a lot of attribution for $210,000!!!!!"

I felt like someone slapped me in the face. In the years that I'd been researching the Morrises, I had begun to feel as if I was their guardian, a protector of their story and legacy. I wanted to find this jerk of a lawyer and ask him how much he had donated to the Southampton library, and then while he was trying to answer, I would knee him in the groin for all those extra exclamation points. His arrogance and high-handedness were beyond annoying.

I read a few more pages of faxes and decided that he was an outlier—a rogue attorney with an attitude. Everyone else—to my relief—was extremely polite and grateful for the Morris sisters' donation.

One of the pages of paperwork said that Robert Berkowitz

would take care of the necessary tax documents and that he would need to approve the donation. There was a paragraph that read, "Interests of the family were education and information. For example they established scholarships for gifted children to attend college. They have helped libraries in other places. They are particularly interested in children."

Elsewhere in the file was a written proposal of what the Morris sisters wanted to donate and what the money would be used for, which the Southampton library rejected. It seemed that the library wanted to move toward digitization and it needed more money than the Morris sisters wanted to donate. Nine months later there was another proposal from the sisters that offered to donate another hundred thousand dollars, which the library board approved.

The second donation proposal was for the naming of the conference room and dedicating the handicapped lift in the Children's Library to the memory of Malvina Morris. It said, "This will give access to the mezzanine level in the Children's Library for children in wheelchairs or those who are otherwise unable to climb stairs. The lift meets all the building codes and requirements of the Americans With Disabilities Act."

After Malvina died in January 1994, Marcella must have been thinking of the best way to memorialize her beloved sister and had come up with this tribute. Within the family, it was said that Malvina and Marcella were the sisters who were closest. And everyone told me how sweet Malvina was. When I saw her name by the handicapped chairlift—a small plaque just above the elevator call button—I was startled to find a lump in my throat. This lift was here because of one sister's love for another, which prompted me to recall a story from Claire.

"I remember when Malvina had cancer of the throat. I went to Southampton to pick up Marcella so we could go to the hospital in Manhattan to visit Malvina and then she would stay overnight with us. You could see that Marcella just could not function without Malvina. They had a very nice home attendant, but it wasn't like her sister. You know when someone elderly loses a spouse? So first, she puts a few dirty *schmattas* [clothes] into a cardboard valise. I decided to take her back to my house so I could wash her clothes and have her shave her hairy chin and upper lip and take a shower, so she could look good for her sister and the doctor.

"When we got to the hospital we met with the doctor first alone. He wanted to operate and take out Malvina's voice box, but I was not going to let that happen. Marcella was very anxious, so I didn't say anything. We then went to visit Malvina. She's in her room and they had put a hole in her voice box to aspirate it. I looked at her and there is this lit cigarette dangling out of the hole. I then said to myself, no surgery. She lived ten more years."

AFTER I LEFT the library, Mattie and I decided to drive to the Gin Lane address where the sisters had lived starting in the 1970s. As we did, we talked about the time in the 1990s when we drove to the house that Mattie, my mother, and their sisters grew up in on

Tyndall Avenue in Riverdale, a swanky part of the Bronx. When we got to the house, Mattie wanted to see inside but she was too scared to knock on the door, so I said we would go together. We walked up the front stairs and I rang the bell, and then I turned and watched as Mattie ran back to the car. I was so surprised that I didn't know what to say when the resident, an old Italian woman who didn't really speak English, answered the door. I explained what we were there for, and the woman agreed to let us see the house. Mattie came back and we had our tour. It was just as Mattie remembered it, smaller than I imagined but pretty and homey. As we stood in the sun porch, I punched Mattie in the shoulder.

I thought a lot about Mattie and my mother and their other two sisters and how close they were, though they never lived together and all very much had their own lives. I've always thought that there is definitely some magic about four sisters. Maybe I've read *Little Women* too many times.

The Morrises' Southampton house had been torn down long ago, but according to my cousin David Green, it was nothing special. (He is the son of Ruth, Bobby and Claire's sister.) David said when he was a kid and his family would visit the Morris sisters, the house would be thick with cigarette smoke. He said everything was sepia toned because decades of cigarette smoke—all of the sisters smoked, David told me—had stained the furniture and the walls. He remembered that the house felt dark and there was no sense that you were near the ocean, even though the beach was within walking distance. When he was in college, David took a summer trip with friends to the Hamptons. He said that he called Marcella and asked if he could come and see her, and she said, "Sure, you want to show off your rich relatives?" He said the remark made him so angry he almost didn't go. The Morris sisters were many things, but no one used them to show off.

Claire told me another story about when the Morrises were living in Southampton. "I was down in the Keys and I got a call from Marcella telling me to come back to New York and out to their house as soon as possible. I asked her what was wrong. She told me her neighbors were planting bushes on her property. Well, I had to go up north to find out what the story was. Not very happily, I flew to New York and went straight out to the Southampton town hall to find out what was going on, and I brought a copy of Marcella's deed. It seems there is a law in Southampton stating that if you put bushes or plants on property other than yours and it abuts your property, in seven years it transfers to you. Smart! But not smart enough for the Morris sisters." Marcella was always ready to fight for what was hers.

THEIR HOUSE WAS torn down not long after Marcella died in 1997. Though I was told that theirs was an ordinary-looking house, the address of Gin Lane was tony: It is now one of the most sought-after streets in one of the most exclusive towns in the Northeast.

When Mattie and I drove up to the address, all we could see from the street were tall hedges and a big iron gate, and behind it a long driveway. I found an online listing for the current house on the property and read it out loud to Mattie: "The house was built in 2007 with eight bedrooms and eleven bathrooms, and it has 9,500 square feet. The house last sold for $2,300,000 in January 1998. The estimated value of the house in today's dollars was more than $18 million.

"More than $18 million," I repeated for emphasis.

Mattie asked, "What should we do?"

"We should ring the doorbell and tell them you grew up here."

We did nothing of the sort. Instead we tried to peek through the gate and hedges to try to get a glimpse of the house, failed, got back in the car, and headed back to Montauk. As she drove, Mattie berated me (or really my father) for not cozying up to the Morris sisters when he had the chance. I was angry, too, but not about any lost money or inheritance. I was thinking about what I could've asked them about their lives but never had the chance. Oh, the party in 1980. I can't begin to tell you how many times I've wished to go back to that place and just ask her and Malvina all the questions. "Hi, Malvina and Marcella, in forty years I'm going to be obsessed with you and I will need to get some details and facts about your life if you wouldn't mind." Sadly, I was too young and not me yet and they were old ladies and an opportunity of a lifetime was missed. Also, I wish I had bought a two-bedroom apartment on the Upper West Side at that time, when it was cheap, and now I'd be living like a queen. Again, I had no forethought. Children, pay attention!

EVEN THOUGH I ordered all the Morris sisters' Social Security applications at the same time, they came one at a time over several weeks. I think that's because the Social Security Administration has a flair for drama.

The first to arrive was Malvina's, and I was excited to see her handwriting on the application. It was dated December 21, 1936, and it listed her address as 29 Charles Street, New York, NY. She was working at Sobel Brothers at 150 Duane Street, downtown. Her age, thirty-six; date of birth, 11 March 1900; place of birth, "Roumania"; sex, female; race, white; father's name, "George Bernard Morris"; mother's maiden name, Schneirer; and below that was Malvina's signature. Not much new information, but what I found encouraging was that these were hard facts, and facts are the building blocks of truth. More research revealed that Sobel Brothers was a shoe company whose headquarters was on Duane Street, and Malvina was the company's bookkeeper.

The next application to arrive was Selma's. Hers was dated December 14, 1936, which suggested that all of the sisters applied together. It said, "Unemployed at Present," and it also listed her address as 29 Charles Street. Her age, forty-two; date of birth, 15 December 1893; place of birth, "Focsini Roumania," sex, female;

race, white; father's name, "George Bernhart Morris," mother's maiden name, Schneirer; and below that was Selma's signature.

I remembered what Herbie said about Selma: "Selma! Never! Stopped! Talking! Ever! She had a mouth like a machine gun and could drive everyone in the world batshit." He added, "If you're trying to measure up who was the biggest wacko of the sisters, she was, you know, premier, in my opinion."

I told him that was not something I was going to measure, and truthfully, I think wacko is in the eye of the beholder.

Claire had told me she thought that throughout her life Selma carried a heavy burden and a lot of guilt. After all, at seventeen she watched her father put her mother in an insane asylum and her younger sisters into an orphanage several months later. Claire told Selma there was nothing she could have done to prevent it, but Selma believed that she should have been able to stop some of it or at least make it easier for her sisters to understand. I told Claire that Selma was just a kid herself, but Claire reminded me that wasn't how they considered you at seventeen in the early twentieth century: Many women were married at seventeen. Including two of my mother's sisters.

"I don't know if you know this, Julie, but Selma was very pretty and had a beautiful singing voice," Claire said. I had seen pictures of Selma as a teenager and she was quite lovely: long wavy brown hair, large dark eyes, and a perfect bow mouth.

Claire continued, "She was also very bossy. She got a job with Sears and Roebuck in St. Louis selling washing machines. She traveled door-to-door." She stopped, and the expression on her face changed. "Did you know that one of her good friends was Golda Meir? She told me this! I didn't believe her until she showed me a letter Golda Meir had written to her. If I remember, Golda wanted Selma to join an organization in St. Louis and then go to Israel."

Claire said that Selma would've gone, too, but she was very dedicated to her family. "She took it upon herself to make sure that everyone was okay. When Marcella and Malvina were older and able to take care of themselves, they grew to hate her interference," Claire said. According to every member of my family, Selma's defining characteristic—other than talking nonstop—was her really annoying personality. Despite that, the three of them lived together.

While I believed Claire, I also wanted to confirm that it was possible that Golda Meir and Selma Morris could have known each other, let alone been good friends. Having learned the hard way that Marcella never worked with J. P. Morgan, I didn't want to make the same error twice.

I was able to learn that though Golda Meir was born in Kiev, Ukraine, in 1898, she emigrated to Wisconsin in 1905 to escape the pogroms. How she and Selma might have gotten to know each other remains to be seen, but they were close in age, both Jewish immigrants who had settled in the Midwest.

Claire continued. "I don't know if you know this, Jul, but your great-grandmother had a lot to do with the life of the Morris sisters. When they left the orphanage, they decided to go to New York to find family. Your great-grandmother Martha took them in. She also took my mother in. That's why I know so much about the Morris sisters and why your grandmother, my mother, and the Morris sisters were so close. They were like sisters." I had no idea about this, and it made me feel much warmer toward my great-grandmother.

"Selma was the one who had the closest attachment to their mother; she always went to visit her," Claire said. This was the first I had heard that any of them had gone to see her. "In the late 1940s, when they were all in New York, Selma went back to St. Louis to be near her mother till she died in 1953."

This detail caught my attention, because in my deep dive into the life of Golda Meir, I learned that Meir had actually been in St. Louis in 1948 and 1949. It was possible she and Selma could have met after all, as Selma was listed on her mother's death certificate (incorrectly as Thelma) as being present and with a St. Louis address.

On Selma's own death certificate, when she died in May of 1991 in Southampton, her occupation was listed as a salesperson for washing machines.

WHEN MARCELLA'S Social Security application finally arrived, I ripped it open at the mailbox to see where she worked, only to find that the government had made a mistake: The information was for the wrong Marcella Morris. I called the Social Security helpline and spoke to the most confused government employee who ever existed, and after talking with him for an hour, I decided it was worth it for my mental health simply to pay another twenty-five dollars and order the application again. This time it came much faster and was correct, but it turned out to be not as informative as I had hoped. Much of Marcella's information was the same as Malvina's and Selma's—the address of 29 Charles Street, her place of birth, her gender and race, and her parents' names (except spelled differently). Her business was listed as Reliance Advertising at 444 Madison Avenue, which was in Midtown Manhattan near Rockefeller Center. So this was 1936 and she wasn't in a financial firm yet. I knew that Harold Bache took over from his uncle Jules Bache in 1944, so she would have been his secretary sometime after that.

I was disappointed that Marcella's Social Security information wasn't the golden key I was looking for, but I had done as much as I could as a regular person, not a historian, and I was going to have to be okay with that.

I'D ALMOST FORGOTTEN that I was waiting for Ruth's application when it arrived. Hers was dated the following June of 1937 (I imagined her older sisters nudging her to do it). She was the only sister who didn't live at 29 Charles Street. Instead her address was 257 West Fourth Street, which is about a ninety-second walk from her sisters' home and just around the corner. Claire had told me the other sisters had never let Ruth live with them because she "got a little strange."

She "got" strange?

"Yeah, did I tell you she got married?" Claire said.

I had heard that Ruth was the only sister to get married, but I never found any record of her marriage. I did come across a lot of Ruth Morrises who were married in New York, but they all stayed married and went on to have children. So none of them were my Ruth Morris.

"Ruth was married to a wonderful guy for about two years," Claire said. "Her sisters could not accept him. You know they never liked men after their father abandoned them. And being that the money came from them, they made life difficult for the newly-weds, approving (or disapproving) how they spent money. The couple split up, and that's when Ruth became a little strange. And then the husband died not long after that."

David remembered that Ruth's husband had never gotten a new car. So Ruth made Marcella buy him one, but he died before it came. (The men in that family did not have good luck.)

Herbie told me that Selma, Marcella, and Malvina used to say that Ruth's marriage was the reason she died so young. It was true that Selma lived to almost ninety-seven years old, Marcella to ninety-five, and Malvina to ninety-four, while Ruth died at seventy-three.

When I was growing up, Ruth was the sister I'd heard the most about. She was the colorful one. "The nut," as family members called her, back when people were looser with their descriptions of others.

I told Claire and she said she didn't like that term. "I'll tell you about her and you decide," she said.

Did she have some form of claustrophobia? As Claire had told me that Ruth did not like to live in anything with a roof, that possibility struck me. "She would camp out on Orchard Beach, which is in the Bronx, until she got caught, then she'd go to Brighton Beach or Rockaway. She did that a lot. Or if she was living in an apartment, she would sleep on the fire escape. I don't know where she got her money, maybe Marcella, because she traveled all over the world. She told me that the Arab men were the best lovers." Claire arched an eyebrow. "She said they would anoint you in oils after the loving.

"One time, must have been around 1970 or so, Ruth called and asked me to come to her apartment. She said she had something that would just fit into my house." Claire shook her head. "I didn't want to go because she lived on Riverside Drive—you know, up where it's not good, where you lived?"

I said I knew exactly where she meant.

"She insisted I come. I got my girlfriend to go with me for protection. When we got there and parked we saw these scary men hanging out of windows, sleeping on the street, and sitting all over the porches. I said, 'This is it, we are in trouble.' The men seemed to be in a stupor, so we decided to take our chance. We proceeded up the front steps of the building Ruth lived in, went into the lobby, and rang her bell. We saw by the apartment number that she lived on the third floor. There was no way we were going to take an elevator in that building, so we walked up the stairs, huffing and puffing, three flights. We got to her door, which was open—we thought she must have heard us coming. When we got in the apartment we noticed all her windows were open, too. I remarked about it. Her answer was, 'They come in to rob me every day. If I leave everything open, they don't break the locks and the windows.'

"We looked around. Jul, she must have had thirty-six couches and forty-two tables and chairs. It was like a furniture showroom or the home of those crazy men who kept all those newspapers." (She meant the Collyer brothers, notorious hoarders from the 1930s and '40s who were crushed to death by their belongings in 1947.)

"I said to her, 'Ruth, what is this?' She told me they were all antiques and she was storing them until they were sold. She had a couch in the bathtub. I said to my friend, 'It's time to go,' but Ruth insisted I see the gift she had for me. It was a gigantic marble and metal table that you see in hotel lobbies. There was no way I could or would take that. She insisted. I said I would have to send a mover to get it. I never did.

"Another time she called to ask if she could store a very expensive rug in my garage. Jerry"—Claire's husband—"was not happy about it. He didn't know what it was, and he knew Ruth. It was delivered all rolled up and papered. I had it put in the garage and waited and waited and waited for her to have it picked up. Finally, I called Ruth and said, 'What's with the rug? The moths are going to eat it!' She told me to wait some more because she didn't want to pay taxes for it—she lived in New York and we lived in Jersey. I think I waited a year and finally I said, 'I've had it!' So I opened the paper—and what was there? No rug, just the under padding of a carpet! I threw it out and Ruth never mentioned it again.

"At one point, Marcella bought Ruth a house in Patchogue. She lived there with a couple; they paid rent to her and she slept on the beach. I was concerned for Ruth, so I asked Marcella why she was allowing this. Her answer was, 'Should I put her away like Mother?'

"Ruth died shortly after that. I am really angry at myself for not taking some things from the house. But who knew? Eileen, Bobby's wife, took two paintings and had them framed. They look beautiful. Every time I go to her house I want to steal one. How would they know?"

(I remembered seeing a painting by Malvina there, a beautiful vase with flowers, but never one by Ruth.)

I told Claire that it sounds as if I would've loved Ruth.

"You would have, Jul."

I asked Claire if she thought Ruth was different from her sisters because she was not just the youngest, but the only one born in the United States.

"You know, I think that's probably true. She saw herself as very modern, and Marcella, Selma, and Malvina were old-fashioned, like the old country. They felt very far apart in age, even though it wasn't that much."

When I looked for a work address on Ruth's Social Security application, I saw her business listed as "The Federalist Theater at 122 E 42nd Street." I gasped.

I'd studied Franklin Delano Roosevelt's Works Progress Administration (WPA) in college. In 1935, FDR signed an executive order to create the WPA as part of his New Deal to help lift the United States out of the Great Depression by providing jobs for the legions of unemployed Americans (unemployment levels at the time were at a whopping 21 percent). In 1938, 3.3 million Americans worked for the WPA. A big part of the WPA was creating infrastructure jobs for unskilled people, but it also oversaw something called Federal Project Number One. These programs employed artists, musicians, actors, and writers across the country to perform for people and create art. Today, the WPA murals are some of my favorite works of American art. You can see them in many public places around the United States. The first one I saw was in a local post office when I was a child. I've seen several in New York City post offices.

Roosevelt intended Federal Project Number One—or Federal One, as it was called—to put artists back to work to inspire and entertain the public. One of the programs, the Federal Theatre Project, under the direction of Hallie Flanagan, created theater troupes for out-of-work actors and writers. (There is a 1999 movie about it written and directed by Tim Robbins called *Cradle Will*

Rock, with Cherry Jones as Hallie Flanagan.) The idea was to create a national theater that produced quality productions that would educate and engage audiences in social issues.

So Ruth worked for the Federal Theatre Project as a writer. This revelation made me happy because she had continued to be creative after her lovely high school stories. And it was a significant achievement to be at that theater at that time.

I knew that some of the Federal Theatre Project's plays are kept in a collection at George Mason University in Virginia. I contacted the library and was able to order a copy of Ruth's play *Affidavit*. When it arrived, it came with a cover sheet from the National Service Bureau WPA Federal Theatre Project, whose address was listed as 1697 Broadway, which is now the Ed Sullivan Theater. It said:

The NATIONAL SERVICE BUREAU was organized primarily to secure and develop dramatic material of the highest standard for Federal Theatre Projects throughout the country. The BUREAU now offers a similar service to Little Theatre groups, community and school theatres and amateur and professional drama organizations.

Among its varied functions will be found the following:

Publication of lists of outstanding ROYALTY and NON-ROYALTY PLAYS for all occasions. These lists of recommended plays contain complete analyses, source information, important director's notes and suggestions for production:

Among the published lists which contain a wealth of highly recommended plays are:

Anti-War Plays, Catholic Plays, Children's Plays, Christmas Plays, Easter Plays, Historical Plays, Irish Plays, Jewish Plays, Marionette Plays, Musical Plays, Negro Plays, New One-Act Plays, Religious Plays, Thanksgiving Plays, Vaudeville Sketches.

It sounded like the script of a radio announcer from the era.

What had been sent to me was a photocopy of Ruth's one-act play. I loved looking at the typewritten pages—all fourteen of them, single-spaced, the lines not perfectly straight, the punctuation thick. *Affidavit* is about a dastardly doctor who tries to get a union member to stop participating in a community hospital fund (like health insurance) because the doctor claims those "community types" are trying to steal this worker's money from his paycheck for nothing. Then the good community doctor enters the action and says the worker is free to do what he wants, but the little money he puts into the fund will save him money if he or his family ever needs to go to a hospital. The bad doctor then tries to get the worker to sign an affidavit, but the worker can't read, which gives the good doctor the chance to explain why the bad doctor is really trying to sabotage him. The laborer says he needs the money now and can't put it toward a future emergency, when suddenly there is a crash outside. A truck has hit a little girl, and the little girl turns out to be the laborer's daughter. In the bad doctor's hospital, taking care of his possibly crippled little girl would cost the laborer $500, but since he's been paying for this community hospital, his daughter's treatment is free. And scene.

The play, though short, has a lot of stage directions like "shame facedly" and "eyeing him suspiciously," the characters' faces "hardening" and "softening" and "betraying wrath." I loved it and would've read twenty more of Ruth's plays if she had written that many and if they were available.

I thought again about the family story that Ruth had written the script for *High Button Shoes* and that a producer had stolen it from her. It was a popular Broadway musical in the 1940s and was later produced on TV. The comedy was based on a book by Stephen Longstreet (whose real name was Chauncey Weiner, possibly the greatest name ever).

It didn't make sense to me that a script by Ruth would've been stolen from a work based on a novel that she didn't write. The book was called *The Sisters Liked Them Handsome*. I bought a copy of the novel from a used book dealer, and it didn't take me long to realize that *High Button Shoes* was not the work that had been stolen from Ruth Morris. I did additional research of theater notices for Ruth Morris from 1930 to 1945 and found two different news items in *The New York Times*.

NEWS OF THE STAGE

October 26, 1936

Ruth Morris has written one called "the Lowells Talk Only To God"; all about the introduction of the factory system in this country. "Behemoth" also by Miss Morris is in circulation again after having been held by Alex Yokel and James R. Ullman. . . .

(Alex Yokel and James R. Ullman were successful theater producers in the 1930s.)

NEWS OF THE STAGE

September 7, 1937

Without any immediate presentation in sight, The Actor's Repertory Theatre nevertheless is pondering a few items for production when and if. For instance, John O'Shaughnessy and Fred Stewart are dramatizing "Washington Jitters" the Dalton Trumbo novel which Moss Hart was once supposed to be adapting. Ruth Morris has submitted her comedy, "The Lowells Talk Only To God" (which, however, needs rewriting), and other items under consideration are a revival of Eugene O'Neill's "The

Straw" and a one-acter named "The Homeless." These are in addition to the already noted plan for a commercial production, in association with John Houseman and Orson Welles, of "The Cradle Will Rock."

The names of Ruth's plays helped me get to the root of the *High Button Shoes* saga.

From what I was able to piece together, in 1956, Ruth saw a notice in *The New York Times* for a televised production of a play called *Bloomer Girl* (confusing bloomers and high button shoes totally makes sense to me). It was being televised by NBC. She filed a lawsuit, claiming that her work had been stolen by the producers of *Bloomer Girl*. It took until 1960 for the suit to go to trial in the Southern District of New York, and Ruth appeared pro se (legalese for defending herself).

I tracked down the judgment and had to read it several times before I understood it.

> The alleged offending work is a musical play, "Bloomer Girl," which was performed from September 1944 through June 1947, in the United States and Canada and was a box office success. It was based on "Evalina," a play by Dan and Lilith James, written in 1943.
>
> The defendants herein are Fred Saidy, one of the librettists of "Bloomer Girl," who adapted it from "Evalina," E.Y. Harburg, the lyricist of the musical compositions of

"Bloomer Girl," John C. Wilson, one of the producers of the musical, and the National Broadcasting Company, Inc., which televised an abbreviated version of it in May 1956. Dan and Lilith James, named as defendants, were not served. However, all individual defendants, whether appearing herein or not, have denied under oath that they knew or ever heard of the plaintiff or her play until the commencement of this suit, almost thirteen years after the original presentation of "Bloomer Girl."

Plaintiff herself does not claim that she ever met any of the defendants or delivered her play to any of them. She does, however, contend that her play was purloined by one of them and that "Evalina," on which "Bloomer Girl" is based, "bears resemblance to my play The Lowells * * *, while the said libretto and lyrics [of "Bloomer Girl"] parody and burlesque, and copy the entire substance of my said drama, * * * that the great bulk of the copying from my said work—scene by scene, sequence by sequence and line by line—was done by said librettists and lyricist."

The plaintiff, since she appears pro se, was permitted to testify in narrative form in support of her charges, and also to meet the defense of laches.

The plaintiff acknowledges that she has no direct evidence of access to her play by any of the defendants. She relies upon what she terms circumstantial evidence, and reasons as follows: In August 1942, after her play had been rejected for production by the Erwin Piscator The-atre Group in New York City, plaintiff left a copy with a young lady on the Group staff, whose name then was, and still is, unknown to her, who stated that she would try to have the play produced at Smith College or some other women's college. Shortly thereafter, in December of that year, a play by Dan James was produced by the same Group. According to plaintiff, playwrights tend to "hang around" studios or theatres while their plays are in re-hearsal. From this premise she infers that James followed custom and was around the studio during rehearsals of his play. She then makes the flat charge that on such an occasion James picked up the copy of "The Lowells," which she had left with the unknown staff member of the workshop. Thus, without foundation of established fact, inference is built upon inference to reach the conclusion of access. The charge of the theft of the copy of her play by the defendant James is most implausible and fails for lack of proof.

To support her charge, the plaintiff submitted upon the trial a 371-page exhibit entitled "Annotation," where-in is set forth in one column selected portions of her play, in the second parallel column, alleged similarities and identities in "Bloomer Girl" and in the third column, historical references to Mrs. Amelia Bloomer and Bloom-erism.

I have studied the Annotation with its alleged pin-pointing of copying of plaintiff's play, and have also read the scripts of plaintiff's play and "Bloomer Girl." The plays are wholly dissimilar in plot, theme, incident, language and characters. The dissimilarity is so marked that there is no real basis for comparison. A great many of the alleged similarities or identities which plaintiff purports to find and which are paralleled in the Annotation are strained, forced or nonexistent.

"The Lowells," as described by the plaintiff, is a serious historical drama of a sociological nature. It is a story of New England factory labor, as well as the beginnings of the feminist movement. Indeed, it is significant that nowhere in the extended Annotation is there a single instance of a copying of a sentence or a paragraph, despite the fact that such is one of her charges.

Finally, great stress is placed upon alleged similarities in environmental factors. Thus, plaintiff points out that her play takes place in Lowell, Massachusetts, a New England industrial town, and the "Bloomer Girl" in an eastern industrial town; that demonstrations or flare-ups occur on the town green in each and that the rather proper boarding house in "The Lowells" is parodied by the former bordello in "Bloomer Girl." The extremes which mark plaintiff's attack are evident from one item, typical of many others, which she contends gives substance to

223

her charges. In her play she describes a bedroom in the company-owned boarding house which has colored woodcuts of "The Cotter's Saturday Night," Raphael's "Madonna" and "The Last Supper," and then charges as a similarity that "nude pictures play an important part in the wall decor" of the former bordello in which The Lily, the newspaper, is published by Dolly Bloomer.

Purported similarities of a like nature, in support of her charges of access and appropriation, are set forth ad infinitum in the Annotation, but no purpose would be served by a discussion of each. Suffice to say they do not sustain the charges.

The plaintiff has subjected "Bloomer Girl" to a microscopic dissection, but even this labored effort has failed to justify her extravagant charges. The two plays just bear no resemblance—at least not to this average reader. They are so unlike that it is difficult to understand how she could persuade herself that the one was borrowed from the other. Particularly appropriate to the instant case is a statement by our Court of Appeals in an earlier case:

"In order to suppose that these * * * authors should have found in the plaintiff's play cues for the farfetched similarities which she discovers, one must be obsessed, as apparently unsuccessful playwrights are commonly obsessed, with the inalterable conviction that no situation, no character, no detail of construction in their own plays can find even a remote analogue except as the result of piracy. 'Trifles light as air are to the jealous confirmations strong as proof of holy writ.'"

The Court concludes that upon all the evidence the plaintiff has failed to sustain her burden of proof and that the defendant is entitled to judgment of dismissal upon the merits.

The foregoing shall constitute the Court's findings of fact and conclusions of law. Morris v. Wilson, 189 F. Supp. 565, (S.D.N.Y. 1960).

Imagine how much time Ruth spent creating an annotated 371-page exhibit and filing the lawsuit. I tried to find the actual documents of the suit but could not. I'm sure it would have made for interesting reading, yet it was clear she had no case.

Again it struck me that the Morris women did things that women weren't known for doing. They witnessed their mother be institutionalized and concluded that their father was a weak man who had destroyed their family. They forged their own paths and refused to let society dictate what they could and couldn't do. They went out into the world and pushed for themselves in a society dominated by men, and by many measures they succeeded. Even when they didn't, their failures were because they had forged their own paths.

NINETEEN

Last Wills and Testaments

W hen Alison, my researcher, was working with me, we tried to track down the sisters' wills. We learned that if you mailed a request to the county records office, it could take months to get an answer, but if you went in person, you could get the documents you wanted right away. It was a tactic several genealogists had suggested, so I asked Alison if she wanted to come with me to Riverhead, Long Island, where the Suffolk County records are kept, to help me track down the Morris sisters' wills. She agreed.

A day before we were to go, my child got sick and I had to stay home and be the ministering angel. Alison said she had an uncle she would like to see in the area so she went by herself. Several hours later she texted me that she had gotten copies of Marcella's,

Malvina's, and Selma's wills, but that Suffolk County did not have a copy of Ruth's.

Of course, I was completely unsurprised. Nothing about the Morris sisters' story was ever nicely packaged and simple. To my amazement, I was less upset about this than I might have been had I known what I was looking for in the wills.

Several days later, a huge package from Alison arrived at my apartment with the wills inside. I flipped through them quickly and then set them aside with other piles of research that had overtaken my desk (and by desk, I mean the living room coffee table). As the months went by, I moved the package from place to place, and then one day I was talking to my friend Ann about trying to figure out how to get the sisters' death certificates. Ann suggested I contact the Reddit genealogy group, as someone on it might have ideas on how to do that. I had already posted a few questions I couldn't find answers for on Reddit and had gotten some replies, but nothing that made it seem I'd missed something I should have known, which was the worry that plagued me throughout this process.

When I posted my query about how I might track down the sisters' death certificates, one responder said, "Too bad you don't have the wills."

That was when I became the emoji with the bulging eyes.

I opened the wills and behind the first page of each of them were Marcella's, Malvina's, and Selma's death certificates. And that was when I knew it was bad that Ruth's wasn't available.

Selma died in 1991 at age ninety-seven from cardiac asystole after years of coronary artery disease. Malvina died in 1994 at the age of ninety-four of myocardial infarction after years of arteriosclerotic heart disease (she also had emphysema). And Marcella died in 1997 at the age of ninety-five of respiratory arrest and metastatic cancer. Pretty ripe old ages for all of their chain-smoking and eating what they wanted for more than seventy years.

The death certificates also listed their last jobs. Selma sold washing machines at Famous-Barr department store in St. Louis, which had been a very long time ago, before she moved back to New York, but this must have been what Marcella and Malvina remembered. Malvina's last job was as a bookkeeper at Wanamaker's department store in New York City, while Marcella's had been as a self-employed commodities broker.

Selma's will was pretty thin, and like her two sisters, she specified that she wanted her remains to be cremated. Why had they chosen to be cremated? Cremation wasn't really done in Judaism at the time, though it is more common today. Was it because none of them had husbands or children or many close relatives or friends? If you don't think anyone will visit your grave, it might feel pointless or even humiliating to have one. I kept thinking about the Alastair Sim version of *A Christmas Carol* when Scrooge sees his grave: A haunting, desperate feeling always comes over me. Then I remembered Clara's and Guerson's graves in St. Louis, and all of the graves we saw in Romania, how little attention future generations paid to them and how lonely they seemed. Maybe the sisters had a point.

· · ·

MALVINA MADE HER last will a few years before Marcella did, but the wills were nearly identical. They left all of their money to a few family members (none of whom was me) and the rest of the will was a detailed list of financial holdings. These were the pages that made my eyes glaze over. I really had no idea what I was looking at, and then I realized the last columns were the value of each holding at each sister's death. When I tried to look at them more carefully, the numbers made me freeze. There were so many aspects of the Morris sisters and their lives that impressed me, and Marcella's genius with numbers was right at the top of my list. When I was a kid in the 1970s, girls were not encouraged in the areas of science or math or even business. Marcella had been a kid sixty years before I was, when no one was encouraging girls to do anything but get married and have children. Her excelling in the world of high finance—in commodities and investments—could not have been easy. I realized that despite all of the research I'd done about her, I still wasn't sure of the exact path Marcella took, or the ups and downs she experienced. But looking at her finances at the time of her death showed very clearly one truth: that she was as successful as everyone always said.

Translated into today's dollars, and after expenses were taken out, Marcella left an estate valued at close to $10 million.

TWENTY

Saying Goodbye

W hen I was a kid, I would pray at night. It had nothing to do with being Jewish or our family's religiousness, it had to do with seeing kids praying at night on TV. They would kneel by their beds and pray for something really heartbreaking— to get adopted by their foster parents or for the family dog's cancer to be healed. They never prayed for a trip to Disneyland or anything crass. Being the savvy kid that I was, I figured that I should start praying before I needed something, otherwise I would come across to the Almighty as a sycophantic opportunist.

I imagined God hovering above my house in a sort of 1960s pie-plate-style spaceship. He looked like he did in Michelangelo's *Creation of Adam* painting on the ceiling of the Sistine Chapel, but kinder—sort of God crossed with Santa. In my mind's eye, I could see him through the wide windshield of his spaceship, steering, looking down on all of us, his subjects.

In the ship with him were all my dead relatives. He was flying them around heaven and every night they'd take a pass over our houses. (My religious perceptions were heavily influenced by the Rankin/Bass Christmas productions.) I would pray not for things, just for him to take care of my dead family. And I would end every prayer the same way: "I hope you are having fun in heaven." I wanted God to know I cared not just about the dead people, but also that he was taking some time for himself. #Godcare.

As I got older, I prayed less to the Guy in the Sky and more to the one who watched that my checks didn't bounce more than once. My praying took place at the ATM, the mailbox, and the answering machine. But I still thought of my relatives up there in the spaceship, and when friends died, they joined my family up there, too.

During the times when life was difficult, I imagined them all up there waiting to hear what I needed. I didn't close my eyes and clasp my hands, it was more like active thoughts as I walked around. "Grandpa, please make someone offer me an assignment before my rent is two months late." Or, "Grandpa, please help my kid get through my divorce without too much pain." I pretty much only ever ask my one grandpa, my mother's father, Saul. I was the closest to him, but he was also the one who was most likely to take care of what his family needed. From a kid's point of view, he had a seemingly endless supply of money, he was generous with it, and when I had a problem or needed help, he would put his arm around me and say, "Whaddaya need, puss?"

When I started writing this book, the spaceship added four more passengers: Selma, Marcella, Malvina, and Ruth Morris. At first my view of them was sort of vague because I didn't really know them individually, except that Marcella was the sister who made all of the money. Mostly I was asking for them to help me find the answers to the questions I had about them and their lives. When I found an answer or uncovered a fact, no matter how small or inconsequential, I would look up to the sky and send them kisses and thank-yous.

When I finished my travel for this book—to Southampton, Romania, St. Louis, Hyde Park, Ellis Island, and Greenwich Village— and I found all the research I could unearth, I felt a pang of disappointment for the many details I couldn't find. And I had a lot of regrets. I really wished I could have found out why Clara had been committed to the asylum, and learned how Marcella managed to become self-employed, who Ruth married and what happened to him and their marriage. And what about the stories of the White House and Golda Meir? There were so many facts I found along the way that I found fascinating: Ruth's playwriting, Sam's life in Texas and his parallel experiences to his sisters, that the sisters had traveled all over the world. They took ships and planes, sometimes together and sometimes alone. Selma, for example, went to

Rotterdam in 1955, and a few days before my husband and I left for a vacation to Portugal, I found Marcella's TWA ticket from New York to Lisbon in 1960. Such background didn't really help me piece together the sisters' larger story, but seeing the ticket made me understand that these women weren't constrained by their marital status or their gender. They had had unfortunate and difficult starts in life, but those tragedies—a mentally ill mother, a father who abandoned them, years spent living in an orphanage—didn't define them. Rather, they propelled them.

I was talking about them with my dad one night and he told me how unusual he thought they were when he was a boy: He wasn't sure if it was because they were the only unmarried women he knew or because they were such strong, independent women. I told him that what captivated me about them and their stories was how much they persevered and succeeded and that they were women! I went from being interested in them as subjects to write about to loving them as unique, dynamic women I was proud to be related to.

At a funeral a few years ago I listened to the rabbi talk about the deceased's five children and his many grandchildren. "We all come from somewhere—the people before us—we never really do anything by ourselves," he said.

Growing up, I mostly identified with my mother and her sisters. They were strong but they were taken care of by men. My mother's mother calculated her four daughters' value in how well they did at finding husbands with financial means. That was part of me as a child, though when I started therapy at age eighteen, I was very aware it isn't exactly a healthy or useful attitude for women to have.

My mother's father worked in his father-in-law's mattress ticking factory, Solinger and Sons, along with his two brothers-in-law. When my mother's older sisters got married, their husbands went to work there as well, along with her male cousin. There were seven incredibly smart female children of my grandfather and his brothers-in-law who were never even considered as employees for the company. My mother, aunts, and I have often talked about how it never occurred to anyone in their family—men or women—that the daughters would come into the business. What the women could have done with it and how the company might have thrived was fascinating to think about, particularly as their one male cousin ran the company into the ground not that many years after he took it over.

My father's mother worked with a jewelry designer in New York City's diamond district when my father was young. She was a businesswoman! But my dad felt that her absence from home while he was growing up destroyed his childhood, and he was completely against my mother working outside the home until my brothers and I were in high school (though to be clear, there was no job my mother was burning to do until then). My grandmother told my mother, her daughter, that if a woman worked, it meant her husband wasn't able to support her. (I know, I know, but it was in another time and under other circumstances.)

Because these ideas were perpetuated through generations of my family, working women weren't part of my identity growing up. I knew some women who had careers, of course—friends of my parents—but mostly I saw mothers who stayed at home or worked part time to "help out." Those women's lives were tied to their families and their homes.

Even after I graduated from college and started working, I didn't really believe that I could support myself or a family. I always thought I would add to some future husband's income. I would make the "mad money" while my husband made the real money that would buy us a nice Manhattan apartment—maybe a Classic Six—and keep us comfortable. When I found myself actually having to make enough money to support my child years later, I did it, but it never felt like me. It felt like Cinderella looking at herself in her rags: You knew that she was meant to be in princess clothes. I couldn't help but feel that I was posing as a functioning, responsible adult but I really wasn't: I should be keeping house and being the junior partner to my husband, who was making the money that sustained us in our comfortable, secure life.

This changed for me when I went from having jobs that I struggled to shoehorn myself into to finding work I enjoyed that I felt capable of doing well.

One of the amazing and unexpected benefits that I realized when I researched the lives of the Morris sisters was that they were identified as my relatives. When I would tell people about them and what I was learning, their reactions made it clear that they thought I was part of them. I was proud of this relationship, and had a sense of competence I'd never felt before. I was connected to a group of strong women who did what they did and succeeded without the support of men. They were the complete opposite of the conventions and attitudes of my mother's family. And somehow, I feel as if I'm a quilt made from them all.

I also realized that while technical difficulties prevented me from writing this book fifteen years ago, I wasn't really ready to write it then. I couldn't have understood at that point in my own life just what obstacles the Morris sisters overcame and how deeply difficult their choices were to make in 1920. I see that those same decisions would be difficult for me to make in 2020.

As I researched this book, my coffee table became Morris sisters central. I had a file for each sister and one for all the major places they'd lived. For three years my family wasn't allowed to put anything else on the table (they did anyway, but it was technically a breach of regulation).

When I finished the manuscript, I took all the files and papers about the Morris sisters and put them into one tall pile and just stared at it. And then I began to feel sad, desperately sad. Normally when I complete a draft of whatever it is I'm writing, I do a happy jig and schedule celebratory lunches/drinks/dinners with as many friends as possible. But this time my reaction was different. I didn't want to leave these women; I didn't want to be done spending time with them.

I walked around for about a week with a sadness I couldn't get away from. It was like mourning. It felt like a death somehow—or four deaths. I wanted to go back to Romania and St. Louis, and rent an apartment on Charles Street. I wanted to spend more time with the Morris sisters, getting to know them bit by bit, fact by fact, as I'd done for the past three years.

And then I realized that there had been a death in me, too. The person who thought it was her birthright to be incapable of self-sufficiency, the woman who expected the world to be predictable, reliable—she was gone. I no longer saw myself that way. After all, I was related to the Morris sisters, Selma, Malvina, Marcella, and Ruth—women who dealt with life on their terms and lived and loved and survived by carving out a place for themselves in the world. And understanding that truth made me feel different—renewed.

I think that we all have a need to find out where we came from, and invariably there is some history, some truth, that explains who we are to our own satisfaction. Some of us reject it and make a different path for ourselves. And some of us embrace these notions and put them on display for everyone to see.

In the beginning, I was fact-checking the history of the Morris sisters that I'd heard from my family, and so many times I felt deeply disappointed to be thwarted by the lack of proof that there had ever been a White House visit or a copy of the letter from Golda Meir or a handkerchief from J. P. Morgan. But despite those tantalizing, missing details, what I am left with now—and what I can share with my family, too—are their lives. Like why their father put them in an orphanage, and what their mother suffered through, and what it took for these four sisters to get where they got. What made them, each in her own way, difficult and wonderful, annoying and confident. How a person like Marcella could have this truly storybook life arc, from being born in a country that doesn't want her to walking a thousand miles across Europe to crossing an ocean in steerage to losing her mother in the worst imaginable way to gathering her sisters in New York to making $10 million—every bit of it entirely on her own, through nothing but sheer will and stubbornness and, yes, maybe some meanness. It doesn't matter whether or not she slept with J. P. Morgan or advised FDR. It doesn't matter that *High Button Shoes* wasn't stolen from Ruth. What matters is these four sisters forged an incredible life out of almost nothing, and they are *my* cousins.

I found this all in the facts, yes, but I also found it in the helpfulness of Viki and Larry in St. Louis, the knowledge and care from Mr. Rond in the Focșani synagogue, the good humor of Valentin, the doggedness of Alison, the cooperation of the people in Southampton. I feel like this army of helpers I assembled along the way became a profound part of all this. I didn't really know what I was doing, and I learned a great deal more in part through the goodness of a lot of people.

I HAD A DREAM a few weeks before I completed the research on the Morris sisters. In the dream, I was sitting at a long table next to my mother, and at the other end were the Morris sisters, all of them very old. I asked my mother what I should do and she said, "Go talk to them, this is your only chance!"

My thought was that this was my opportunity to find out what happened to their mother, what happened with Ruth's marriage, and whether Marcella really did go to the White House.

I got up from my seat and walked to the other end of the table. As I reached them, I saw that they got younger and younger until they were in their forties—my age. They were laughing and chatting with each other, Ruth dressed as a flapper and singing "It's Only a Paper Moon" as Malvina got up to dance around the room, her legs strong and fine. Even before I spoke I realized that I wasn't going to get the answers to my questions, and that maybe I should just leave them alone to enjoy this time together.

At that point, Marcella noticed me and said, "What do you want, Snoop?"

"I have questions," I said.

She smiled at that and, shaking her head, she looked at her sisters and said, "We were very good at hiding the evidence."

Afterword

Having been in therapy for more than thirty years, I know that your dreams are written by your brain. The dream I'd had about the Morris sisters was not likely a visit from them. They have other things to do, I'm sure.

I also know that the truth about the Morris sisters matters much less to me now than I thought it would. When I started looking into their lives, I was certain that the truth about them would be found in straight, clear facts. I was wrong. What mattered—what I learned was true—was that spending time with them, getting to know them and growing to love them, is now part of my life and will be forever.

THE END.

. . .

WELL, NOT QUITE.

I finished writing this book and it was on its way to production (when a book is copyedited and its layout is set). I was quite pleased with everything, recalling the years of hard work that I'd put into it and all that I had discovered. Basking in my glory, if you will. I decided that it was maybe even better that I didn't get all the answers to my questions about the Morris sisters, because for most people, that is how their search into the past will go: Some questions will be answered, other questions will pop up, and if you pay attention, you'll learn something from both. And people should feel fine about that. Life isn't a movie. The stories in it don't always get tied up with a neat bow.

My editor and his assistant were going through the photos that I wanted to use in the book. He noticed that one of them had a funny mark on it and asked if I could submit a clean version.

This turned out to be a complicated request. I had found the photograph on Ancestry.com, which I had subscribed to during the time I was doing research for this book. When I finished the research, I kept my Ancestry subscription for another month but then ended it, which meant that I couldn't retrieve the photo without resubscribing to the site.

I called my friend Ann and asked if she could locate the photo for me: She is an avid Ancestry user and would never close her account. Early on she had made a Morris family tree on Ancestry to convince me to write the book, so she went to that and searched for Ruth to locate the photo. As she did, she asked me several questions about Ruth, and I told her I could never find Ruth's death certificate or any information on her marriage. I had looked for three years. I explained that sometimes you just need to be okay with a brick wall.

Ann's response was simple: "Huh," she said.

I said, "They were married for a short time, then they split up, and he passed away shortly after that. Probably from a broken heart. There are no records."

Ann said, "His name was Paul Koditschek, and they were married September 30, 1942."

Long pause.

"What?"

"Yeah, it's right here," Ann said. "It looks like the record was recently added."

She texted me the image of the marriage license. It said:

Paul Koditschek, white male, born on 11 April 1911 in Vienna, married Ruth Morris 30 September 1942
 Residence: 130 Bank Street, New York, NY
 Occupation: Statistician
 Father: Seigfried Koditschek
 Mother: Elsa Koditschek
 The witnesses were Erika and Edward T. Zusi
 Marriage Certificate #15772

I looked at the image, and tears leapt out of my eyes. I really did wonder if I was dreaming again. I was so flustered I kept saying, "Oh my God, oh my God." She went on. "Well, he didn't die right after they split up because he died in 1974," she said. "I guess his heart wasn't that broken," she said as, at the other end of the phone line, I restarted my Ancestry membership, shaking as I entered my credit card number.

"Wow," I said, counting in my head. "He was seven years younger than Ruth was."

"And he got married again," Ann said. "In 1948. Oh wait—he was in the military—"

"Okay, I'm logged in—where are you?" I said.

We were like two detectives, one dumb and one smart, each pursuing the same case. One moving very fast and the other moving . . . the opposite of fast.

At last I tracked down Paul Koditschek in my Ancestry search. The first detail I saw was his draft card.

"Okay, we are going back," I announced.

Digging back into Ancestry.com, I found the ship's manifest of when Paul arrived in America. He left Cherbourg, France, on the *Queen Mary* and landed in New York on March 23, 1939. His occupation then was listed as lawyer and he was twenty-seven and single. His draft card was dated October 1940. Jeez, the military didn't give him time to catch his breath.

A year later he filed an application for naturalization called a declaration of intention. It said he lived at 36 West Tenth Street and worked as a manager, and that he came from Vienna, Germany. (For those of you who remember *The Sound of Music*, Austria was annexed to Nazi Germany in 1938. It was called the Anschluss and it cut short Maria and Captain von Trapp's honeymoon.) At that time Ruth was living on West Fourth Street and Malvina, Marcella, and Selma lived on Charles Street, all very close together in the West Village. West Tenth Street was just a few blocks away.

Ann said, "I bet they met at a café!"

I was Google-Mapping the locations when Ann said, "Wait! What date did they get married?"

"September 30, 1942," I said.

"He enlisted in October. October 1942 until October 1945."

"What? That was less than a month after they were married!" I said as I located the document Ann was looking at.

"Maybe she was a war bride!" Ann said dramatically. "And I bet Paul was a spy!" She told me about how the US Army used native-speaking Germans as spies. Apparently Henry Kissinger did this.

We moved over to Fold3, a military records site. There we learned that Paul had enlisted at Fort Jay on Governors Island as a private.

More searching and we found that Paul was in the army from October 20, 1942, until October 27, 1945. But he hadn't been sent back to Europe to spy. It looked as if he was stationed in the Admiralty Islands in New Guinea in 1944 and became a naturalized US citizen there.

I was squinting at the tiny type on the ancient forms when Ann said, "Ohmigod."

"What? *What?*"

"Hold on, I'm emailing you something."

"What?"

"Paul's mother is famous!"

A few seconds later an email from Ann appeared. I opened it and clicked on a link to a *New York Times* piece from 2018 with the headline "The Nazi Downstairs: A Jewish Woman's Tale of Hiding in Her Home."

The story was amazing. Elsa Koditschek had lived in her home in a prosperous area of Vienna near the foothills of the Alps when her house was confiscated by the Nazis and an SS squad leader moved in. At first Elsa—who was Jewish—was permitted to stay, but it wasn't long before she received a deportation edict from the Nazis, ordering her to move to a Jewish ghetto in Poland. Instead of obeying the order, she snuck away and hid in the homes of some of her non-Jewish friends until she managed to sneak back into her own house and hid there until 1944 when the Allies bombed Vienna. She finally escaped to Bern, Switzerland, where she lived for the remainder of her life.

The point of the article was that before World War II, she had bought a painting called *City in Twilight* by the Austrian painter Egon Schiele and it was lost to the Nazis. Sotheby's got involved in getting the painting back to the Koditschek family, and in the process discovered that there were boxes of letters from Elsa to her son, Paul, written throughout the war. The letters proved the provenance of the important Schiele painting, which was great. But what about the provenance of Ruth's husband?

Elsa at age forty-three had decided to purchase the remarkable Schiele landscape. She was the widow of a banker, who in early 1939 saw the Nazis approaching and sent her son and daughter away to safety. It was both brave and farsighted, and I bet Ruth thought so, too. This extraordinary, heroic woman had briefly been her mother-in-law.

THE ARTICLE MENTIONED Paul's granddaughter, Sarah, and I managed to track her down. I contacted her and told her who I was and that my relative had been married to Paul Koditschek from 1942 to maybe 1946 (I never could find a divorce record). I believed he was her grandfather and wondered if she knew anything about his first marriage.

She replied right away: "Oh, interesting. I did research on my grandfather, so it's funny you ask. That marriage was kind of a mystery to me, so you might know more than I do. Want to talk and see if we can piece anything together?"

I called her and we chatted for about forty minutes. When we spoke she was a reporter living in Little Rock, Arkansas. I filled her in on all that I knew about Ruth, and she told me her grandfather had had a girlfriend in Vienna who became a famous photographer, which led us to think that he must have been attracted to artsy girls. She told me that she would talk to her father and uncle and asked me what I wanted to know from them. I told her I would like to know what Paul did in World War II, where he was stationed, what jobs he'd had over the course of his life, and if they knew anything about his marriage to Ruth. And if there were any photos, I would love to see them. And I wanted to know what he had been like when he was a young man. I knew that would be the hardest question of all to answer.

Sarah told me she would see what she could find out and would get back to me.

That night I couldn't fall asleep. I kept thinking that Ruth had sent me this information, and in a very dramatic way. I thought of how many times I'd asked for this information from the Morris sisters, be they angels or ghosts.

The next morning, I heard back from Sarah.

1) What did Paul do in the army?

He was in the artillery, in the Pacific Theater, since the army wouldn't allow recent immigrants like him from German speaking areas to fight in the European Theater, even though they presumably knew he was Jewish.

2) What job did he hold after the war?

After the war, he was a statistician, holding various insecure jobs until he found a position as an inventory control analyst at Avon Products in the mid 1950s—a job he held until his death in 1974.

3) Did you know anything about his marriage to Ruth?

We knew nothing of his marriage during his lifetime. Ted, his son, discovered it after his death and tried to talk to his mother about it. She was certainly aware of it but knew little about it, or chose not to be forthcoming.

As far as we know, there are no photographs of her, or of them together.

4) What was he like?

Paul was a left-progressive in political terms. At the time he was an Austrian émigré who was involved in the Resistance against the Nazi Regime. He was also interested in art and avant-garde ideas of the kind that were circulating around Greenwich Village in those days.

. . .

SO THERE IT WAS. Answers—which always brought more questions. How did they meet? Why did they get married right before he enlisted? Why were they married for such a short time?

Since my knowledge of Ruth and Paul as a couple was so limited, I decided that they had been wildly in love and that the marriage was an act of passion. Paul was a handsome refugee who had fled the Nazis and was interested in the arts. Ruth was a pretty, free-love-espousing, bohemian socialist and playwright.

Though Claire had thought Paul died right after he and Ruth had split up, that might have been more metaphorical than accurate. She did remember him as a sweet guy, and I'm sure that she was right when she said that the sisters meddled in Ruth's marriage. But it appeared that Paul had been stationed abroad for most of their marriage.

Paul Koditschek

No one really knew what happened, but I was glad to learn that Paul had gone on to live a happy life and that he didn't die of a broken heart without getting his new car.

Sarah and I communicated a bit more, reiterating how miraculous this all felt and how hard I had struggled to find this information.

"I actually consulted a medium," I said, "that's how desperate I was!"

"Wow!" she said. "What did you find out?"

"Not much," I told her. "It was a couple of weeks before Trump was elected, so I guess the ghosts were a little busy with that."

Sarah said she would pass along any photos or letters that mentioned Ruth or the marriage if she came across them.

AFTER SARAH AND I said goodbye, I reflected on the exciting coda to the Morris sisters' story. I realized that these family search stories often have a stopping point, but they never really end. This book is over, but I have no doubt that in the years to come I will hear from people who know some fact about one or all of the Morris sisters, a detail that I missed, or who will point me to an archive that has just the information I was looking for when I wrote this. My search, like families, could go on forever.

But I'm finished. For now.

I think.

Acknowledgments

———◦———

Since I published my last book, Esther Newberg, my agent, married my husband and me. I think that's all I need to say.

This is my sixth book and they've all been published by the team at Riverhead Books—there is no better place on earth and I'll fight anyone who disagrees with me. Thanks to the A-Team: Jake Morrissey, Geoff Kloske, Jynne Martin, Ashley Garland, May-Zhee Lim, Molly Fessenden, Amanda Inman, Kate Stark, Lydia Hurt, Jacqueline Shost, and the magnificent sales department.

Deepest thanks and admiration to Viki Fagyal, the St. Louis Genealogical Society, Larry Harmon, Kevin Lake, Elizabeth McDonald, Diane Everman, Beth Gates, Erin Warnke, Mircea Rond, Alison Fairbrother, Estie Berkowitz, Angelina Krahn, Sarah Whites-Koditschek, and Valentin Georghe.

Love to my cousins for answering all my calls, especially Robert Berkowitz, Eileen Berkowitz, Sherie Wolpert, Carole Krinsky, Geraldine Velasquez, Sandra Khaner, David Green, and my Unky Hoib (Herb Khaner).

More love and thanks to Ann Leary, Meg Wolitzer, Laura Zigman, Claudia Glaser-Mussen, Patty Marx, Alexandra Mayes Birnbaum, Barbara Warnke, Kristin Moavenian, Adam Resnick, Molly Jong-Fast, Dorothy Warnke, Lydia Butler, Pari Berk, Lauren Gilbert, Jancee Dunn, Susan Roxborough, Vesna Jovanovic, Sam Maser, Martha Broderick, Mattie Matthews, Brian Klam, Matthew Klam, and Ellie Davenport.

David, I am so proud to be your mom and love you so much.

Dan Davenport, you're the cream in my coffee.

In loving memory of Claire Manowitz.